Walking in the Word

60 Days to Being Transformed by God's Truth

Andrew Wommack

All emphasis and brackets within Scripture quotations are the author's own.

Published in partnership between Andrew Wommack Ministries and Harrison House Publishers.
Woodland Park, CO 80863 – Shippensburg, PA 17257

ISBN 13 TP: 978-1-59548-818-3

ISBN 13 eBook: 978-1-6675-1582-3

For Worldwide Distribution.

1 2 3 4 5 6 / 26 25 24 23

Psalm 139:14–16

I will praise thee; for I am fearfully and wonderfully made: marvellous are thy works; and that *my soul knoweth right well. My substance was not hid from thee, when I was made in secret,* and *curiously wrought in the lowest parts of the earth. Thine eyes did see my substance, yet being unperfect; and in thy book all* my members *were written,* which *in continuance were fashioned, when* as yet there was *none of them.*

None of us evolved or just came into being accidentally. Whether our parents planned our birth, or regardless of how we were conceived, the Lord knew all about us from the moment of conception.

The Hebrew word *rāqam* was translated "*curiously wrought*" and was translated "embroiderer" and "needlework" in other scriptures.[1] It's designating deliberate and skillful action. The *Amplified Bible* translates this phrase as "*My frame was not hidden from You, When I was being formed in secret, And intricately* and *skillfully formed [as if embroidered with many colors] in the depths of the earth.*"

You were planned by God!

Verse 16 goes on to say that all the days of your life were written in a book before you saw the light of day. That does not mean whatever happens to you, good or bad, is from God. No! But God had a plan written out for every day of your life before you were even born.

The Lord created us free moral agents, but His plans for us are only good (Jer. 29:11). He doesn't force His plan on us. Each of us has total freedom of choice (Deut. 30:19). But the right choice is to find out God's plan for our lives and submit to it.

He created us for a purpose, and our greatest potential is only realized when we follow His plan. The good news is, God wants to reveal His plan for our lives to us more than we want to know it. If we seek, we will find (Matt. 7:7) when we seek with all our heart (Jer. 29:13).

Seek the Lord's plan for your life today. He will answer and show you great and mighty things which you know not (Jer. 33:3).

Psalm 139:16

> *Thine eyes did see my substance, yet being unperfect; and in thy book all* my members *were written,* which *in continuance were fashioned, when* as yet there was *none of them.*

Notice the first part of this verse where God saw our "*substance, yet being unperfect.*" The literal meaning of the Hebrew word *golem*, which was translated "*unperfect,*" literally means, "a wrapped (and unformed mass, i.e. as the embryo)."[2] When you were still in the embryonic stage, the Lord saw your substance.

Compare that with Hebrews 11:1, which says, "*...faith is the substance of things hoped for, the evidence of things not seen.*" So, it was God's faith that produced your substance while you were still an embryo in your mother's womb. The Lord has never created a failure or someone to merely exist, and He never will. His plans for you are awesome!

Romans 11:29 says, "*...the gifts and callings of God* are *without repentance.*" That means that God's purpose for your life never changes. Just as a GPS device takes whatever wrong turn we make and recalculates to get us back on track, the

Lord can take whatever mess we've made of things and use it for His glory (Rom. 8:28).

Ask the Lord today to show you His original plan for you and then expect Him to reveal it. If you are already following His will, then ask Him to show you where you are along that path. We need to keep His original vision in front of us and not turn to the right or left. Examine yourself to see if you are where He wants you to be (2 Cor. 13:5). He is willing and able to help you make any corrections necessary.

Jeremiah 1:4-5

Then the word of the L*ORD came unto me, saying, Before I formed thee in the belly I knew thee; and before thou camest forth out of the womb I sanctified thee,* and *I ordained thee a prophet unto the nations.*

What the Lord spoke to Jeremiah in this verse confirms what David wrote in Psalm 139:16 about the Lord having a plan for his life before he was even born. Paul said the same thing in Galatians 1:15.

God's plans for our lives were determined before we were born, which clearly reveals that the Lord didn't choose us based on our talents and abilities. Rather, our talents and abilities were given to us at birth to accomplish a specific, God-given purpose. We can hone and develop those abilities, but we can't put in what God left out.

The key to godly success is discovering what that God-given purpose is and then devoting the rest of our lives to accomplishing it, regardless of the cost. We might achieve some level of success in our own strength, but we will never reach our true God-given potential until we submit to His plan for our lives.

When we stand before the Lord, He won't reward us according to what we accomplished in our own strength. Regardless of how many awards or trophies we have on our mantel, the Lord will deal with us based on what His plans for our lives were and how we fulfilled them.

God loves us more than we can ever comprehend. His plans for us are better than the plans we have for ourselves (Jer. 29:11). True happiness lies in discovering and submitting to God's will and plans for our lives. Make today count for eternity.

1 Corinthians 3:12-15

Now if any man build upon this foundation gold, silver, precious stones, wood, hay, stubble; Every man's work shall be made manifest: for the day shall declare it, because it shall be revealed by fire; and the fire shall try every man's work of what sort it is. If any man's work abide which he hath built thereupon, he shall receive a reward. If any man's work shall be burned, he shall suffer loss: but he himself shall be saved; yet so as by fire.

Remember from yesterday's devotion that the Lord won't reward us according to what we accomplished in our own strength. He wrote a plan for us in His book before we were born (Ps. 139:16), and we will be rewarded according to how we fulfill His plan. We might attain success in the eyes of men, but when we stand before the Lord, He will judge our works according to His plans, not ours.

The gold, silver, and precious stones represent works originating from and accomplished through the Holy Spirit. The wood, hay, and stubble represent our own works, whether good or bad, done independently of the Lord. The metals will be purified by the fire, but the wood, hay, and stubble will be burned up. And notice this verse says the Lord will try every man's work to see what sort it is, not what size it is.

There will be Christians who were esteemed in the eyes of men, but when the Lord sets His purifying fire to their works, they will be reduced to ashes. Only what was done in the Lord's strength and according to the Lord's will, will stand the test. Every deed done by our own design and in our own power will be burned up.

This doesn't mean Christians will lose their salvation. Paul went on to say that they "*shall be saved; yet so as by fire.*" This is talking about our rewards, not our salvation. Salvation is dependent on Jesus and faith in Him alone. But who wants to stand before the Lord and find out their whole life was contrary to God's plan for them? We need to keep in mind that this life is not all there is. We will live for eternity, and there will be a reckoning before the Lord to see how well we fulfilled our God-given purpose.

Each day, we are either moving forward in God's plan and goals for our lives or we are just wasting this precious gift of life. This is not a dress rehearsal. Today is a gift from God. Make it count.

Day 5

Jeremiah 1:6

Then said I, Ah, Lord God! behold, I cannot speak: for I am *a child.*

This was Jeremiah's response to the word of the Lord, which told him that before he was born, he was sanctified and ordained to be a prophet to the nations (Jer. 1:5).

I had exactly the same response when the Lord called me to preach. I told Him He must have made a mistake. I was an introvert and was terrified of speaking in front of people. I just couldn't do it.

But the Lord doesn't see things the same way that we see them. I was evaluating myself based on my natural tendencies, not on what He saw in me. The Lord not only calls, but He also equips those He calls. God doesn't call the qualified; He qualifies the called.

We serve a BIG God who has big plans for each of us. I often tell people, "If you feel sufficient to do whatever it is you are doing, then I doubt you have found God's true purpose for your life." The Lord will call you to something that is beyond yourself, so you will have to depend on Him.

First Timothy 1:12 says that when the Lord called Paul into the ministry, He counted Paul faithful. Paul wasn't faithful at that time. He was anything but faithful. He had been the persecutor of Christians, even consenting to their death. Do you realize that most of the Bible was written by men who had killed people (Moses, David, Solomon, Paul)? That means there is hope for you and me. The Lord has never had anyone qualified working for Him yet.

But God saw Paul, not as he had been, but as he could be in the future. God has a plan for us, and it's better than we could ever imagine. If God believes in us, all we must do is get in agreement with Him. We can do anything He calls us to do when we are letting Him live through us.

Jeremiah 1:7

But the Lord *said unto me, Say not, I* am *a child: for thou shalt go to all that I shall send thee, and whatsoever I command thee thou shalt speak.*

The Lord told Jeremiah that he was called and separated to be a prophet to the nations while he was still in his mother's womb (Jer. 1:5). Jeremiah said there was no way that could happen. He was just a child and couldn't speak (Jer. 1:6). The Lord told Jeremiah to never say that again. He would go to all the Lord sent him to, and he would speak the words the Lord put in his mouth.

This same thing happened to me in January of 1973. I knew I was called to the ministry and had tried to minister for two years, but it was painful. I was so introverted that I couldn't speak in front of people. I memorized three messages for my first three-day "revival" meeting and was so nervous that I preached all three messages in five minutes on the first night. It was terrible.

But in January of 1973, as I was agonizing over a commitment I had made to minister in front of 300 people, I couldn't sleep. I got into the presence of the Lord and lay on the floor of our first little apartment for hours. Finally, the Lord spoke

Jeremiah 1:9 to me, where He touched my mouth and put His words in my mouth. He coupled that with Jeremiah 5:14, which says, "*Wherefore thus saith the* L*ORD* *God of hosts, Because ye speak this word, behold, I will make my words in thy mouth fire, and this people wood, and it shall devour them.*"

Suddenly, I knew it wasn't me speaking anymore, but it was Christ speaking through me (Gal. 2:20). My fear left, and faith came flooding into me. Now, several decades later, I've let the Lord speak through me to billions of people worldwide. If it works for me, it will work for you in whatever endeavor the Lord has called you to (Rom. 11:29).

Determine today to quit speaking out your fears and instead draw on God's power inside of you. You can do all things through Christ who strengthens you (Phil. 4:13).

Philippians 4:7

And the peace of God, which passeth all understanding, shall keep your hearts and minds through Christ Jesus.

There is a peace that passes all understanding when you are in the center of God's will for your life. That's one of the ways you can know you are where you are supposed to be.

For sure, there are times that our dissatisfaction or depression is the result of our own bad choices and actions. But it's also true that there is a holy dissatisfaction that comes from God when we are not doing what the Lord has called us to do. Regardless of how much we pray for peace and desire it, nothing substitutes for being exactly where the Lord wants us to be.

I once spoke with an Asian woman who was a receptionist at a friend's business in Charlotte, N.C. She asked me what I did, and I told her I was a minister. She got all excited and said, "For who?" I told her I was a minister for the Lord Jesus Christ. She went wild.

She told me that the night before, she was going through her Buddhist rituals when she just stopped and cried out to God. She said she knew He was real, but this couldn't be the right way to connect with Him. She asked the Lord to reveal Himself to her. A ball of light came right up to her, and she heard a voice say, "Tomorrow, I will send you a man who will tell you who I am." She said, "You must be the man!"

I said, "I am the man!" I got to lead this woman to the Lord, and she was gloriously saved. Praise the Lord!

But you know, one of the greatest things about that experience for me was knowing I was in the right place at the right time. I knew I was exactly where the Lord wanted me to be. There is no other feeling like that on earth. There is a supernatural satisfaction that can only be found inside God's will.

If you don't have that assurance that you are doing exactly what the Lord has created you to do, don't waste any more time. Do what this woman did and ask the Lord to reveal His will to you.

Romans 12:1-2

> *I beseech you therefore, brethren, by the mercies of God, that ye present your bodies a living sacrifice, holy, acceptable unto God,* which is *your reasonable service. And be not conformed to this world: but be ye transformed by the renewing of your mind, that ye may prove what* is *that good, and acceptable, and perfect, will of God.*

These are the two verses that "jump-started" my understanding of what the Lord wanted me to be and do. As I neared my high school graduation and contemplated college, I had to make decisions about what I would do with the rest of my life. So, my senior year in high school, I started studying the Bible in earnest, looking for answers. When I came across the last part of Romans 12:2, I knew this was the key.

That verse says if I will do what Romans 12:1–2 instructed, I would "*prove what is that good, and acceptable, and perfect, will of God.*" That's what I had been searching for. I wanted to know God's will for my life. The word "prove" means "to make manifest to the physical senses." I knew the Lord had a plan for my life, but I just didn't know what it was. This showed me how to make God's will manifest to my physical senses.

So, for the next four months, I focused on those verses nearly exclusively. I prayed constantly for the Lord to help me understand what a "*living sacrifice*" was and how I could become one. I also asked the Lord constantly to show me how to renew my mind. I didn't really understand what I was doing, but I had a promise from God, and I was pursuing it with all my heart.

This promise isn't for me alone. This is an open-ended promise to you too. The Lord is no respecter of persons (Rom. 2:11). He wants to reveal His will for your life to you more than you want to know it. If you seek, you will find (Matt. 7:7) when you seek with all your heart (Jer. 29:13).

Take these verses as God speaking directly to you because that is exactly what He is doing. Submit to this instruction from the Lord and resist any desire to do things your own way (James 4:7). Then, get ready for the adventure of your life.

Romans 12:1

I beseech you therefore, brethren, by the mercies of God, that ye present your bodies a living sacrifice, holy, acceptable unto God, which is *your reasonable service.*

One of the first things the Lord revealed to me through this passage was that my vocation is not God's primary will for my life. The number one thing the Lord wants from me is me. He wants me to be a living sacrifice to Him. He loves me more than He loves what I can do for Him.

When I proposed to Jamie, I didn't ask her to marry me because I wanted her to cook and clean for me. I told her I wanted to share the rest of my life with her. She does countless things for me, but that's not the reason I married her. I wanted her, and not just what she could do for me.

Likewise, the Lord wants us more than He wants what we can do for Him. It's important to do what He tells us, but we can't bypass this critical first step. God is love (1 John 4:8 and 16). He wants our love more than our service. If He gets all of us, He will get our service. If we somehow stumble into God's plan for our lives but aren't totally yielded unto Him, we will mess the whole thing up. This happens more often than not.

It's comparable to building a ship. If we skimp on the construction in our eagerness to get out on the ocean, we're probably going to sink. Likewise, the Lord is more interested in making us the person He wants us to be than He is in using us. Preparation time is never wasted time.

The Lord spoke it to me this way, "The reason I don't use you is because you aren't usable. Quit asking Me to use you, and instead, ask Me to make you usable. The moment you get usable, I'll put you to work." Wow! That hurt, but it focused me and set me free.

I promise you that the Lord has a purpose for your life and wants to see you fulfill it more than you do. But He wants you more than what you can do for Him. If He gets your heart, He'll get your service.

Day 10

Romans 12:1

I beseech you therefore, brethren, by the mercies of God, that ye present your bodies a living sacrifice, holy, acceptable unto God, which is *your reasonable service.*

First of all, notice that Paul is begging the readers to present their bodies to God as a living sacrifice because of the mercies of God. It's because the Lord loves you and wants nothing but good for you that He is asking you to surrender to Him. This is not punishment.

One of the biggest reasons people don't commit their lives totally to the Lord is because they think the Lord will ask things of them that kill their dreams or limit all their fun. They are sure that if they were to give the Lord total control, they would wind up in a grass hut in Africa, suffering for the Lord for the rest of their lives. At the very least, they think they will be poor and never succeed.

Although it is true that the Lord's plans for you may not be the same as your current plans, I can guarantee you that His plans for your life are better than your own (Jer. 29:11). He made you for a specific purpose. Everything about you is uniquely suited to that one purpose and plan God created you for. In the center of God's will, there is a contentment and satisfaction that money or fame can never deliver.

If the Lord were to lead you in a direction contrary to where you are currently headed, there would be mercy and supernatural joy, which passes all understanding, accompanying your obedience (Phil. 4:7). He will realign your desires so that nothing else could ever match the fulfillment you get from doing God's will.

This has certainly been true for me, and I know it will be the same for you. The Lord has done for me much greater things than I ever could have done on my own. He has treated me much better than I deserve (Eph. 3:20).

God is calling you to run up a white flag and unconditionally surrender, not to hurt you but to bring you into the true happiness and joy He designed you for. You will never regret it.

Day 11

Psalm 37:4

Delight thyself also in the LORD; and he shall give thee the desires of thine heart.

This verse from Psalm 37:4 reinforces the point from yesterday's devotion, that it's the mercies and goodness of God that compels us to totally surrender to Him. This isn't a promise that the Lord will give us anything we want. That could be misused to ask for many things completely contrary to God's will. This is not a verse to be used to get a new mate, rob a bank, or cheat on our exams.

This is a promise that when we delight ourselves in the Lord (by becoming a living sacrifice), He will put His desires into our hearts. Wow! That totally changes everything. He changes our desires to become His desires.

When you accepted the Lord, you immediately experienced exactly what this verse is describing. Your desires changed. You might not have experienced total freedom immediately. In fact, we are all still in the process of conforming our actions to how we desire to live for the Lord. But when you truly committed your life to the Lord, your desires changed. Even if you still struggled to overcome some individual sin, your desire for that sin changed instantly.

A friend of mine had been sleeping around for years and was actually saved one Saturday night while watching *Saturday Night Live*. They were doing a spoof on the movie, *The Exorcist*. She realized that the demon-possessed woman depicted in the skit was her. She fell down in front of the TV and called out to the Lord to deliver her, and she was miraculously saved. Then she got right into bed with her live-in boyfriend like she had been doing for months.

When she woke up the next morning and saw this man in her bed, she immediately knew it was wrong. She moved out that day. She had been living in that sin for so long, she had become numb to the conviction of the Holy Spirit in that area. But after giving her heart to the Lord (delighting in Him), her desires changed.

Therefore, if surrendering our lives to the Lord changes the direction of our lives, it will be accompanied by the Lord changing our desires so that we will delight in His plans for us more than we ever delighted in our own plans.

Surely, each one of us has experienced this to some degree, and the more we delight in the Lord, the more our desires will conform to His desires for us.

Romans 12:1

I beseech you therefore, brethren, by the mercies of God, that ye present your bodies a living sacrifice, holy, acceptable unto God, which is *your reasonable service.*

What is a "*living sacrifice*"?

It's obvious what it isn't. It isn't doing our own thing and asking God to bless it. Sadly, that's what many Christians are doing today. They are pleading with the Lord to bless what they are doing, but when we are doing what the Lord leads us to do, that's unnecessary. Wherever God guides, He provides. If it's His will, it's His bill.

That's not to say that being in God's will makes everything automatically work out. No. Paul saw a man in a dream calling him into Macedonia in Acts 16, but when he arrived there, it was only days before he was beaten and thrown in the worst part of the prison. Everything didn't just "sovereignly" work out for his best. But the Lord's blessing was on him, and nothing could stop it. The Lord sent an earthquake and released his bonds, and the whole jail was saved.

Paul didn't have to plead with the Lord to intervene and do something. Instead, Paul and Silas were singing praises to the Lord in the midst of a very bad situation. They had that joy and peace that passes understanding that comes from being right in the center of God's will. They were doing what they had been instructed by the Lord to do, and come what may, they were content.

The Lord called and anointed me to minister His Word (2 Cor. 1:21). It's certainly something I can't do in my own power. Remember, I was an introvert and afraid to speak in front of people. The Lord would have been unjust to ask me to do something I'm incapable of doing without supplying His grace and power to get it done. When the Lord calls us to something, there is a supernatural ability from Him to accomplish whatever He leads us to do.

So, today ask yourself this question: "Am I doing what the Lord called and equipped me to do, or am I doing my own thing and asking God to bless it?" I ask that question in my meetings, and it's not uncommon to have 70 percent or more of the congregation stand for prayer because they aren't sure they are doing what the Lord created them for. The answer to that problem is to become a living sacrifice today.

Day 13

Romans 12:1

> *I beseech you therefore, brethren, by the mercies of God, that ye present your bodies a living sacrifice, holy, acceptable unto God,* which is *your reasonable service.*

Let's deal with this once again: "What is a *living sacrifice*?"

For one thing, it's not a one-time occurrence. This is something that has to be living, or a continual process. A living sacrifice has a tendency to keep crawling off the altar. We don't ever reach our goal of being totally committed to God in this life. We move in that direction, but it's a lifelong pursuit.

I missed the Apollo moon landings because I was in Vietnam. I was amazed at the feat of landing on the moon. When I met Jim Irwin, one of the Apollo astronauts, I started pummeling him with all kinds of questions. His answers amazed me.

Instead of them doing everything perfectly, they just blasted off and had a course correction every ten minutes for the four days it took them to travel from Earth to the moon. Then there was a landing strip they targeted that was hundreds of miles in size, but nearly missed. They were five feet from overshooting the designated area. I was shocked. It totally changed my thinking on the whole process.

As I was listening to Jim explain those things, the Lord applied what Jim said to Romans 12:1 about becoming a living sacrifice. We have to blast off, which is to make that commitment to become a living sacrifice, but then we must have course corrections every ten minutes for the rest of our lives.

Just because we have thoughts of exalting our will above God's will doesn't mean we didn't blast off and head in the right direction. It just means it's time for a course correction. The only way we can be totally delivered from our selfish tendencies is to die and go be with the Lord. Our flesh won't bother us then. But as long as we are on this earth, the flesh will seek to pull us back into our own wisdom and understanding like gravity tries to pull everything to the ground.

We can escape the pull of the flesh, but only if we blast off and head towards this goal of being a living sacrifice. We must keep the power at full throttle and make constant course corrections. But it's more than worth it.

Romans 12:1

I beseech you therefore, brethren, by the mercies of God, that ye present your bodies a living sacrifice, holy, acceptable unto God, which is *your reasonable service.*

A sacrifice doesn't have control over what is happening. The offering is at the mercy of the one making the sacrifice. So, to be a living sacrifice, we must yield ourselves totally to the Lord unconditionally. That means no limits and no negotiation.

Carrie Pickett gave this example. She saw herself handing the Lord a piece of paper with all her requests and wanted the Lord to sign at the bottom of the page, validating her desires. Instead, the Lord handed her a blank page and asked her to sign; He would fill in the details. That's totally the opposite of what most of us want, but that's an acceptable living sacrifice.

Think about it. The wage of sin was death (Rom. 6:23). Even though the Lord loved the whole world and did not want us to perish (John 3:16), a holy and just God could not merely look the other way. He couldn't just forgive our sins. The sin debt had to be paid, and by the grace of God, it was.

Instead of extracting the payment from us, the Lord took our sin into His own body and paid the debt we owed (1 Pet. 2:24). He gave Himself as a living sacrifice for us, freeing us from the debt we were doomed to pay. With such a massive sacrifice from Him, it's only reasonable that we should sacrifice everything we are and have to Him. He bought us at a massive price (1 Cor. 6:20 and 7:23). We belong to Him.

But our loving God doesn't extract our sacrifice against our will. We have to present our bodies to the Lord as a living sacrifice. He won't force us to do it. He wants our obedience to come from a heart of love.

So, instead of demanding our submission, He beseeches us to yield from a heart of love. I can assure you of this: the Lord will never let you outgive Him. If you give your life to Him, He will give you back His life flowing through you more abundantly than you could ever think or imagine (John 10:10 and Eph. 3:20).

Run up the white flag of surrender today and get ready to enjoy the blessings of the Lord as never before.

Romans 12:2

And be not conformed to this world: but be ye transformed by the renewing of your mind, that ye may prove what is *that good, and acceptable, and perfect, will of God.*

Being a living sacrifice is actually God's primary will for every single person (Rom. 12:1). But it's only the first step. If we don't renew our minds from the way this world has programmed us, we cannot fulfill His good and acceptable and perfect will for our lives.

Proverbs 23:7 says that our lives are going the way of our dominant thoughts. We can't consistently act differently than we think in our hearts. If we want to change and be like the Lord, we have to change our thinking. We do that through the Word of God.

The word "*conformed*" in Romans 12:2 means "to fashion alike, i.e. conform to the same pattern (figuratively)."[3] You may not realize it, but sin has programmed our thinking contrary to what God intended it to be. Our brains are like computers. The hardware is controlled by software. Our brains function as they were programmed, and we were all programmed incorrectly by the thinking of this world. We were taught to be selfish, angry, fearful, unbelieving, and a host of other things. Even after making the choice to surrender unconditionally to the Lord (Rom. 12:1), it takes time to reprogram our thinking. That's what the Word of God is for.

Second Peter 1:3 says that everything we need for life and godliness comes through the knowledge of God, and verse four says that knowledge is what gave us God's Word. It allows us to partake of His divine nature.

The Bible isn't a book written by men about God. It is a book written by the Holy Spirit through men. It is literally "God-breathed"[4] (2 Tim. 3:16), or as Peter said in 2 Peter 1:21, men "*spake* as they were *moved by*" the Holy Spirit.

The Bible was inspired by God, and it takes the quickening power of the Holy Spirit to make it come alive to you (Heb. 4:12). The Bible is written to your heart, not your head. You have to use your head to read it, but you have to open up your heart to the Holy Spirit to receive its life-giving power.

Renewing our minds is the single most important thing we can do to find God's good, acceptable, and perfect will for our lives. That renewing only comes through God's Word.

Day 16

Romans 12:2

> *And be not conformed to this world: but be ye transformed by the renewing of your mind, that ye may prove what* is *that good, and acceptable, and perfect, will of God.*

The word "*transformed*" in this verse was translated from the Greek word *metamorphoo*,[5] which is the root of our English word metamorphosis, describing the transformation of a caterpillar into a butterfly. If you want to totally transform from something that is ugly and earthbound to a beautiful butterfly that can soar in the air, then that only comes by the renewing of our minds.

When we get born again, our spirits become totally new, but we still have the same mind we had before. The change in our spirits is immediate (2 Cor. 5:17), but changing our thoughts is a process, and like the caterpillar, it can only be accomplished through wrapping ourselves in God's Word until we emerge a transformed person.

Jesus said His words are spirit, and they are life (John 6:63). Since we must worship God in spirit and in truth (John 4:24), the only way we can truly know God is through the truth of His Word (John 17:17). We wouldn't even know how to spell Jesus if it weren't for the Bible. God's Word is His will and reveals His true nature. His nature is now our new nature (1 John 4:17), but we won't know it by just intuitive reasoning. We must take God's Word and exalt it above everything else. That includes the way we were programmed and the way the world is trying to pressure us into its way of thinking.

It's like trying to see what the weather is like outside when you are inside. Unless you can look out a window, it's hard to tell. The Bible is our window into who God is and who we are in our new, born-again spirit. Whatever God's Word says about Him and us is truth, not what we have been brought up to believe.

Outside of Jesus and the Holy Spirit, God's Word is the greatest gift He ever gave mankind. We say we believe the Bible is the inspired Word of God, but we don't act like it. The Bible is God's love letter to us, revealing what He truly thinks about us and all He has provided. But His love letter remains unopened by the vast majority of His children.

Decide today to put God's Word first place in your life. As Romans 3:4 says, "*...let God be true, but every man a liar.*" Let God's Word be the plumb line in your life, and every other source bow its knee to the truth of God's Word.

Romans 12:2

And be not conformed to this world: but be ye transformed by the renewing of your mind, that ye may prove what is *that good, and acceptable, and perfect, will of God.*

Notice that this transformation comes by the renewing of your mind.

Many Christians are desperate and will go to great lengths to beg, pray, and even fast to find God's will. They will go to church, meetings, and conventions all around the world, searching for God and His plan for their lives. Although the Lord can use any of those things, the primary way He reveals His will to us is through His Word. We need to put more effort into the study of God's Word, and it will take care of the rest.

Second Peter 1:3 says that everything we need comes through the knowledge of Him, and then verse four says that knowledge is imparted through His exceeding great and precious promises (His Word). You will never truly conform to the Lord's plans for your life without the revelation that comes through His Word.

God's Word is like the instruction book to a car or any tool. It is put out by the manufacturer to show you how to safely use and get the most out of their product. If you don't use the product according to the instructions, it voids the warranty. Likewise, not following God's instructions voids all the benefits He has provided for us. We need to follow His instructions.

The Bible is God's manual for marriage, health, prosperity, joy, and life in general. Yet few Christians study God's manual. They lean unto their own understanding (Prov. 3:5), which the manual tells us not to do. If something in your life isn't working, look up the proper way of doing things recorded in God's Word and follow His directions. It will work every time.

The single most important thing you can do to find God's will for your life is to study His Word. It's more important than prayer. Prayer is very important, but if we don't study God's manual, we won't know how to pray properly. Our minds have been corrupted by the fallen nature inside, and the only way to think properly is to use the cleansing power of God's Word to reprogram our thinking.

Romans 12:2

And be not conformed to this world: but be ye transformed by the renewing of your mind, that ye may prove what is *that good, and acceptable, and perfect, will of God.*

When we become a living sacrifice, and then get transformed through the renewing of our minds, we will make manifest to our senses the good, acceptable, and perfect will of God.

Notice that we don't immediately come into God's perfect will. It's a process. There is the good and then the acceptable, before we get to the perfect will He has planned for us. It doesn't come all at once. There are stages in finding God's will.

The Lord loves you so much that He won't put the responsibility of His perfect will upon you if you can't handle it. You have to grow into God's perfect will. You must accelerate to go from zero to one hundred miles per hour. If you were to go that fast instantly, it would kill you. That's not acceleration. That's a wreck.

The Lord is kind and gentle with us. He won't put more on us than we are able to bear. If we haven't been faithful in a little thing, He won't give us something greater to do (Luke 16:10–13). He won't give us steps two through ten if we haven't taken the first step.

Also, if the Lord showed us everything He has planned for our lives all at once, many of us would run in the other direction. We couldn't handle it. We would either withdraw in fear or become so impatient that we wouldn't take the time to mature into the person we need to be to fulfill God's will. Preparation time is never wasted time. It takes time to develop the character we need to sustain God's blessings on our lives.

There are some who have stumbled upon God's will for their lives, but they forced it to come prematurely and didn't have the character to sustain the opportunities the Lord gave them. We see this with ministers all the time. You don't want to grow past your integrity.

I knew immediately after my miraculous encounter with the Lord in 1968 that I was supposed to be in the ministry and that it would be big. But I couldn't handle what I'm doing now back then. It's taken me nearly sixty years to grow into the position the Lord has put me in. Thank God He didn't demand what I am doing today from me way back then.

It will be the same for you. Just be faithful with what the Lord tells you to do today, and tomorrow will take care of itself.

Day 19

Mark 4:28

For the earth bringeth forth fruit of herself; first the blade, then the ear, after that the full corn in the ear.

This verse is part of a parable Jesus taught, and it reflects the same truth expressed in Romans 12:2 about steps and stages to experiencing God's perfect will.

In the same way that a kernel of corn doesn't instantly produce a full stalk with ears of corn, likewise, God's Word doesn't instantly produce its full fruit. There is first a little blade that shoots up out of the ground. Then comes the ear of corn and, eventually, the full ear of corn. But it's a process.

We had a man come to our Bible college who had spent his whole life in a mental institution. He was a very nice guy, but had little to no social skills and had never worked a job in his life. He had lived off his family or the government his whole life.

I started encouraging him to believe God for big things, and he took it to heart. He found an old stone hotel that had been gutted by fire and did a whole presentation on how much it would cost to buy, remodel, and then rent it out to our Bible college students. It was pretty impressive.

But when he showed me his plans, I knew it wasn't what the Lord wanted him to do because of this principle of first the blade, then the ear, then the full corn in the ear. He had never worked a job or earned a dime in his life. There was no way he was going to go from that to a five-million-dollar project overnight. I encouraged him to get a job and pay his own rent and living expenses first, and then come back to me with his proposal.

This has become a major revelation to me. We are in a multimillion-dollar building project, but I know I can't do this all in one step. I've cut it up into bite-size pieces and am taking it one project at a time. The old saying is, "You can't eat an elephant all at once, but you can do it one bite at a time."

As you seek to discover God's will, ask Him to show you what your next step should be and do that. If you are looking too far down the road, you could fall over something or step into a pothole. God's will comes in steps and stages, which can only be skipped at great loss to us. The path of the righteous shines brighter and brighter like the dawning of the day (Prov. 4:18).

Day 20

Acts 13:2

As they ministered to the Lord, and fasted, the Holy Ghost said, Separate me Barnabas and Saul for the work whereunto I have called them.

Notice that the Holy Spirit said to separate Barnabas and Saul for the work that the Lord had already called them to. That shows there is time between God's calling and separation.

Knowing God's will is essential, but that's only part of the process of fulfilling God's will. There is a preparation time between the call and the time we are separated to accomplish God's will.

I had a miraculous encounter with the Lord on March 23, 1968, and I knew immediately that the Lord was calling me to serve Him full-time. It took me a couple of years to discover He had called me into the ministry and given me a gift of teaching. I immediately headed in that direction, taking whatever teaching opportunities I encountered.

But after thirty-one years of Bible studies, pastoring three small churches, and then a traveling ministry, the Lord told me on July 26, 1999, that I would just be starting my ministry on January 3, 2000, the day I started my television ministry.

Wow! I was shocked! I had seen wonderful things happen, including salvations, healings, and even seeing people raised from the dead. But the Lord never serves dessert first. If I was just getting started, then something better was ahead.

Sure enough, my ministry took off like never before. I had struggled prior to that time. People were staying away from my meetings by the thousands. But after going on TV, our ministry began to double every few years on a regular basis. More people were being set free than ever before. I learned that there was definitely a difference between being called and then being separated to what God had called me to do.

You may be in that time between knowing what the Lord has called you to do and being separated by the Holy Spirit to accomplish it. That's what I call preparation time, and preparation time is never wasted time. Stay the course. Keep your eyes on Jesus, and He will perfect the good work He has begun in you.

Day 21

Psalm 105:19

Until the time that his word came: the word of the L*ORD* *tried him.*

This passage is speaking about Joseph. The Lord showed Joseph what He ultimately wanted him to accomplish through two dreams (Gen. 37:5-11), but there was a lot of time and difficulties before those dreams came to pass. Until their fulfillment, Joseph's faith was tried by the word the Lord had given him.

Likewise, none of us step into God's perfect will immediately. We have to grow into what the Lord wants to accomplish through us, and you can count on the enemy doing everything he can to steal that vision away (Matt. 13:19). Until the fulfillment of God's plan, we have to stand in faith on what He has revealed to us.

The Hebrew word *tsâraph,* which was translated "*tried*" in this verse, means "to fuse (metal), i.e. refine (literally or figuratively)."[6] Life is a fire, and it will melt you, but the good news is that if you are submitted and committed to the Lord, that fire will only burn up the impurities in you, with the result being a vessel fit for His use.

We've all experienced this. Personally, I went through thirty-two years of serving the Lord before actually starting my ministry (see Day 20). During that time, it was only the word of God, which He had revealed to my heart, that kept me on track. My circumstances didn't match the vision I had on the inside. If I had just gone by what I saw in the natural, I would have quit. There were many well-meaning people who told me I missed God and that I should do something else. But I'm so glad I stuck with the word the Lord gave me. All that time and effort was well worth it.

That was certainly true of Joseph. It was twenty-nine years from the time Joseph received his dreams until he saw them come to pass. That's a long time, but God's plans for us cannot be microwaved. A truly godly life isn't like fast food. It takes time and preparation to accomplish, but the difference between home cooking and fast food is worth it.

The Lord knows that our modern world is built on convenience and instant gratification. But the Lord doesn't change (Mal. 3:6). We must conform to His way of doing things. Patience, which is faith over a prolonged period of time, will make us complete, lacking nothing (James 1:4).

James 1:2-4

My brethren, count it all joy when ye fall into divers temptations; Knowing this, *that the trying of your faith worketh patience. But let patience have* her *perfect work, that ye may be perfect and entire, wanting nothing.*

These verses have been misinterpreted by some to teach that God is the one who gives us problems to make us perfect, but the very context disproves that. James 1:13 says God isn't the one tempting us. If trials and temptations made us perfect, the ones who have been tribulated the most would be the most spiritual. That certainly isn't the case.

However, all of the devil's opposition does serve a purpose. It makes us put into practice what the Lord has taught us in His Word, and as we experience the Word working through us, it makes us stronger.

The military teaches soldiers how to fire a weapon, throw hand grenades, and fight with their hands. However, that's all just theory. A soldier who hasn't actually used those skills is not in the same category as a battle-hardened veteran. It's only those who can translate what they've been taught into action that survive battles.

If a soldier believed that the enemy was sent by his own country to make him better, he would embrace the enemy and probably be killed. No! The enemy only comes to steal, kill, and destroy (John 10:10). But when we resist the devil and see him flee from us (James 4:7), it produces a stronger, tried-in-the-fire faith.

Life is a fire, and it will melt you. You can't avoid the fire. You live in a fallen world, and there will always be opposition. If you never bump into the devil, it's because you are both headed in the same direction. Turn around and follow God, and you are going to experience problems. But the good news is, you get to pick whether the fire turns you into ashes or purifies you.

The choice is yours. I choose to patiently apply God's Word and stand regardless of the resistance. I pray you join me, and together we let God's Word perfect us until we become mature and complete, wanting nothing.

James 1:2-4

> *My brethren, count it all joy when ye fall into divers temptations; Knowing* this, *that the trying of your faith worketh patience. But let patience have* her *perfect work, that ye may be perfect and entire, wanting nothing.*

I think most people think of patience like when we are waiting for a bus. We just sit there and occupy ourselves with "whatever" until the bus arrives. But that's not what the Bible is speaking about when it promotes patience. Biblical patience is an action word. It is defined as "cheerful (or hopeful) endurance, constancy."[7] It's perseverance.

Romans 10:17 says faith comes by hearing the Word of God, and Romans 15:4 says patience comes by the Word. So, I believe patience is faith, but it's faith over a prolonged period of time. It's one thing to have a momentary burst of faith, but it's an entirely different thing to live by faith (Gal. 3:11).

We aren't just waiting on God to do something when we are patient. But we are waiting on God the way a waiter waits on his customer. The waiter is attentive and looking for the slightest indication that his customer wants something. He's not pushy but responsive.

So, a patient person is a person who has a word from God and is attentively seeking the Lord for the slightest indication that He wants something. We aren't forcing the Lord into action. We are just patiently waiting until He gives us a signal, in His own time.

Hebrews 6:15 talks about Abraham patiently enduring in order to receive the promise. The Lord gave Abraham a promise that his children would be as numerous as the sand on the seashore or the stars in the sky (Gen. 22:17). It took decades for that promise to manifest, and in the meantime, Abraham had to patiently endure. He didn't do it perfectly, but the gifts and callings of God are without repentance (Rom. 11:29). That means that regardless of how badly we mess things up, the Lord doesn't change His plans for our lives.

If we will simply hold on to the promise God has given us and patiently endure, it will surely come to pass, just as it did for Abraham. We don't have to badger the Lord to move on our behalf. Just patiently wait for His instructions. They will surely come.

Day 24

Acts 9:10

And there was a certain disciple at Damascus, named Ananias; and to him said the Lord in a vision, Ananias. And he said, Behold, I am here, *Lord.*

This is profound! Ananias was there when the Lord called his name.

The Lord used this scripture to speak to me, and He said, "How many times have I called you, and you weren't there?" Only the Lord knows what we have missed by not hearing Him call our name and give us instructions.

In Ananias' case, the Lord used him to turn Saul into Paul. Paul wrote half of the books of the New Testament. He was the apostle the Lord used to reveal His Gospel of grace, which has transformed countless lives. It's possible none of this would have happened if Ananias hadn't been "there."

Of course, Acts 9:11 follows Acts 9:10. Can I take the liberty to say that if we aren't "there" listening and looking for the Lord, then 9/11 will come? This is an allusion to the terrorist attacks on the World Trade Center in New York on September 11, 2001. Disaster follows us failing to hear what the Lord has to say.

One of the greatest keys to discovering and fulfilling God's purpose for our lives is to simply be "there" waiting on the Lord, instead of being preoccupied with the cares of this life.

The Lord can speak, and certainly has spoken in very dramatic ways, such as in an audible voice, a burning bush, through a donkey, angels, and signs and wonders. But Hebrews 11:6 says that faith is what pleases God. It's the exception, rather than the rule, for the Lord to speak in some conspicuous way. We can miss God's instructions if we aren't paying attention.

The Lord walked on the water to save his disciples, who were close to drowning in a storm. But He didn't do it in a way that they didn't have to exercise faith. He made as though He would have walked by them (Mark 6:48). They had to call out to him before He stilled the storm and translated them to the shore (John 6:16-21).

Likewise, we need to be seeking the Lord and listening for His voice. He is always speaking, but are we always listening?

1 Kings 19:11-12

And he said, Go forth, and stand upon the mount before the Lord. *And, behold, the* Lord *passed by, and a great and strong wind rent the mountains, and brake in pieces the rocks before the* Lord; but *the* Lord was *not in the wind: and after the wind an earthquake;* but *the* Lord was *not in the earthquake: And after the earthquake a fire;* but *the* Lord was *not in the fire: and after the fire a still small voice.*

This was what Elijah experienced in a cave on Mt. Sinai. Elijah had done what no one had ever done before him. He had called for a drought that brought the ungodly kingdom of Ahab to its knees. He called fire down from heaven to consume a sacrifice and killed all the prophets of Baal. He ended the drought by prayer and outran a chariot for twenty miles. He was the first person ever recorded in Scripture to raise someone from the dead. He was used to the spectacular and supernatural.

But after failing God miserably and running for his life, he was in desperate need of hearing a word from the Lord. The Lord sent a wind that was so strong it broke boulders in two. Then an earthquake and a fire came, but the Lord didn't speak to Elijah in any of those dramatic manifestations. It was a still, small voice that brought Elijah to his knees and overwhelmed him with the presence and power of God.

God is awesome, beyond our ability to fully comprehend. He could show Himself in such spectacular ways that we couldn't stand it. I believe that's what the Lord was revealing when He said no man could see Him and live (Ex. 33:20). It's not that He is so private that He will kill anyone who gets a peek. No, it's that He is so Almighty that our bodies can't endure seeing Him. It would kill us.

So, the Lord must hide His full Self from us because our mortal bodies can't handle the full manifestation of His glory. He's left us with many witnesses if we are looking (Ps. 19:1-6), but He has ordained us to know Him by faith.

Just as with Ananias (see Day 24), we must be sensitive to and searching for the Lord's instructions. He won't force Himself on us. He speaks to us in a still, small, inner voice. He never leaves us or forsakes us (Heb. 13:5), and He is constantly wanting to speak to us. However, the sounds of this life are competing for our attention. We have to tune our hearing to the voice of the Lord. Those who have an ear to hear, listen today.

Proverbs 4:20

My son, attend to my words; incline thine ear unto my sayings.

This isn't speaking about tilting our head to a certain angle in order to hear God speak. This is talking about tuning our hearing to God's voice. There are many voices calling out to us every day that compete for our attention. But the voice of the Lord is unique and matches His Word perfectly.

The Hebrew word that was translated "*attend*" in this verse means, "to prick up the ears, i.e. hearken."[8] This is speaking of the way a horse or mule moves its ear to amplify sounds.

I owned horses for many years. I observed how when they hear a sound, their ears can rotate nearly 360 degrees to zero in on that sound. That's what this verse is describing. We have to prick up our ears or tune our hearing to listen to God's voice. He is always speaking, but we aren't always tuned in to His voice.

Old radios didn't have presets or digital tuning. You had to move the dial to receive the signal, and if you weren't exactly on the right spot, the signal would be staticky or gone completely. The signal would also float or fluctuate, so you would have to continually keep adjusting the dial to keep a clear signal.

Likewise, the Lord is always broadcasting His love and instructions to us, but we have to be turned on and tuned in to the right signal. Sadly, we often listen to the devil's signal more than the Lord's. We must incline our ear unto His sayings.

Most radio and TV stations broadcast twenty-four hours a day. If we aren't receiving the signal, it's not the station that isn't broadcasting: it's our device that's the problem. If your TV set goes blank, you wouldn't call the station first and complain about them not broadcasting. The first thing you do is check your set.

Yet, most Christians immediately ask God why He isn't speaking instead of seeing if they are turned on and tuned in. It is never God's signal that is the problem. It's always our receiver that isn't working if we can't hear God's voice. The simple solution is to make sure we are turned on to God and tuned into His Word.

So, prick up your ears today and listen for God's voice. He wants to talk to you more than you want Him to talk to you. It's all a matter of us focusing our hearing so that we recognize His voice above all others. God's word is His voice.

Day 27

Psalm 46:10

Be still, and know that I am *God:*

I had a dream one night in which I saw a big banner that had Psalm 46:10 written on it. Although I had quoted that verse thousands of times, I couldn't think of what that verse said for the life of me. So, I got up and found it in my Bible. I felt like the Lord was telling me to be still and know that He was God.

My wife went into town to shop, so I decided to just sit still out on our patio and see what happened. I believe that being still is more than just not moving, but I didn't want to take a chance. I decided to be as motionless as I could be. I sat still for over an hour. All I did was breathe and blink. I was so still that a chipmunk crawled up my leg, and a deer nearly walked right up to me. It was amazing!

What happened was, I noticed things that I normally wouldn't have noticed. I saw hundreds of ants that were everywhere. There were dozens of chipmunks scurrying around. I could hear the wind blowing through the trees, and there were deer, squirrels, and other critters that were always there, but I was usually too busy to notice. Nothing new was going on. I just became aware of what was around me in a way that I normally wasn't.

I believe the Lord was showing me that just as I was insensitive to what was going on around me in nature when I'm busy, I'm often insensitive to the Lord and what He wants to speak to me or show me because of my busyness. Although He is always with me (Heb. 13:5), I'm not always paying attention.

In order to perceive and respond to God's purpose and direction for our lives, we need to turn down the volume of this world's voices and focus on what the Lord has to say to us through His Word and Spirit. Being in tune to the Lord is much more exciting and healthier than being plugged into this world with all its distractions.

Take time today to be still and recognize the presence of the Lord with you. His plans for you are better than your plans for yourself (Jer. 29:11).

Day 28

Luke 10:41-42

Martha, Martha, thou art careful and troubled about many things: But one thing is needful: and Mary hath chosen that good part, which shall not be taken away from her.

Jamie and I were in Washington, D.C., enjoying all the sights of our nation's capital. As we walked along the mall, I noticed that I couldn't hear my footsteps, although we were walking on gravel. I remember thinking how odd that was.

The next day, we went directly from there to Shenandoah National Park. As I was walking on the Appalachian Trail, I could hear each footstep loud and clear. I remember thinking about the difference between walking on gravel in D.C. and walking the gravel trails in Virginia.

My steps made the same sound in both places. The difference wasn't what I was doing, but it was what was going on around me. The ambient noise in Washington was so loud, it drowned out the sound of my walking. In Washington, there were cars, planes, people, tour guides speaking through microphones, and other sounds that drowned out the sound I was making as I walked those paths.

In a similar way, the noise of this world drowns out the still, small voice of the Lord (1 Kgs. 19:12). I've read that the average American spends over five hours a day on their phones. I know they aren't making calls that whole time. They are surfing the web and letting all the sewage of this world flow through their minds. That can drown out the inner, still, small voice of the Lord.

Like Martha, each of us has duties that need our attention. It isn't wrong to take care of business. But when Jesus is in the house, we should give Him our full attention. Jesus had multiplied food before. He could have done that in that situation too. Martha missed a once-in-a-lifetime opportunity, while Mary was commended by the Lord for sitting at His feet. He said she had chosen the good part, which would not be taken away from her.

Today, make a decision to choose the good part that comes by sitting at Jesus' feet and listening to His words. He will reveal things to you that you haven't heard before.

Day 29

Acts 7:22-25

And Moses was learned in all the wisdom of the Egyptians, and was mighty in words and in deeds. And when he was full forty years old, it came into his heart to visit his brethren the children of Israel. And seeing one of them *suffer wrong, he defended* him, *and avenged him that was oppressed, and smote the Egyptian: For he supposed his brethren would have understood how that God by his hand would deliver them: but they understood not.*

These verses in Acts reveal that Moses knew what God's will for his life was. He defended a fellow Jew, supposing that his brethren would understand that he was trying to deliver them from their bondage, but they missed it. Even though Moses knew God's will for his life, he missed how the Lord was going to accomplish it.

It's not enough to know what God wants you to do. You also have to know God's plan for accomplishing His will and the timing. Moses missed it on both of those counts.

The Lord wasn't going to use Moses' military might or high government position to bring deliverance to the Israelites. The Lord was going to bring such miraculous plagues on Egypt that thousands of years later people would still be talking about it.

Most of us would have made the same mistake Moses did. It was miraculous that his life was spared at birth. One who was doomed to death not only survived but was one of the highest officials in Egypt. Surely, the Lord did all of that to get him into position to bring deliverance to the Jews. It made perfect sense. The only thing wrong with that reasoning was that it wasn't the way the Lord had planned.

Likewise, we often think we know more than the Lord. We get a word from the Lord and make a paragraph out of it. We think if the Lord will just point us in the right direction, we can take it from there. But God's ways are not our ways. We have to trust in the Lord with all our heart and lean not unto our own understanding (Prov. 3:5).

Even if you know God's will for your life, are you following His plans for bringing that will to pass? The ends don't justify the means. We have to submit ourselves to the Lord and follow His plan all the way to the end.

Genesis 15:13

And he said unto Abram, Know of a surety that thy seed shall be a stranger in a land that is *not theirs, and shall serve them; and they shall afflict them four hundred years;*

Exodus 12:40

Now the sojourning of the children of Israel, who dwelt in Egypt, was *four hundred and thirty years.*

Acts 7:30

And when forty years were expired, there appeared to him [Moses] *in the wilderness of mount Sina an angel of the Lord in a flame of fire in a bush.*

Moses' burning bush experience happened forty years after he tried to bring deliverance to the Jews in his own strength and by his own wisdom. If you couple this together with Genesis 15:13 and Exodus 12:40, it becomes clear that when Moses killed the Egyptian and hid him in the sand (Ex. 2:12), he was ten years premature in trying to accomplish the Jews' exodus from Egypt.

So, Moses not only missed the way God wanted to deliver the Jews, but he also missed the timing. There is a time element to everything the Lord wants to accomplish in your life. It's not always a certain date, but there are things that must be worked in us before the Lord opens the doors for us.

The Lord loves us so much that He won't put us in a position we aren't prepared to occupy. He loves us more than what we can do for Him, so He is patient, waiting for us to mature to a place where we can handle the pressures that come with the promotion. Our delays are often related to our immaturity.

That's probably why the Lord revealed His will to Moses ten years before it was time for him to accomplish it. It takes time to grow into the position the Lord has for us. Impatience won't get us to the finish line any quicker, but our impatience can delay God's plans for us. In Moses' case, it cost him forty years in the wilderness, and it cost the children of Israel thirty years of extra bondage.

The quickest way to get into God's perfect will doesn't involve shortcuts, but rather, total commitment to the Lord's will, plan, and timing. If we are seeking the Lord first and foremost, He will get us to the desired location quicker than we can ever get there on our own. Realign your sights on the Lord today and know that He is working to perfect the work begun in you (Phil. 1:6).

Philippians 3:13-14

Brethren, I count not myself to have apprehended: but this *one thing* I do, *forgetting those things which are behind, and reaching forth unto those things which are before, I press toward the mark for the prize of the high calling of God in Christ Jesus.*

Paul wrote this toward the end of his life and ministry. He had served the Lord as few ever have, before or since. He was used of the Lord to take the Gospel to the Gentiles and write half of the books of the New Testament. Yet he still hadn't arrived.

The truth is, none of us totally arrive in this life; we just leave and start moving in the direction the Lord has for us. Our journey won't be complete until we enter into eternity. Paul was still pressing toward the mark the Lord had set for his life at the very end.

The perfect will of God isn't a destination but a journey. We are all moving through this life and are headed in some direction. We are either getting closer to accomplishing God's perfect will for our lives or wasting the most valuable possession the Lord has given us—time. There isn't any other alternative. There is no such thing as just marking time.

We can't get time back. Each day is a precious gift that will never come our way again. So many people are just going through life without knowing for sure that they are moving in the direction that the Lord wants them to go. That's not the way Paul was.

The Apostle Paul said in 2 Timothy 4:7 that he had run his race and finished his course. He had a specific course that he ran. He was headed toward a goal the same way a runner is striving toward the finish line. There was a prize to be won, and he wanted to get it. Paul wasn't just "going with the flow" or reacting to what life threw at him. He had a goal of knowing the Lord (Phil. 3:10) and making Him known (Eph. 6:19).

What are your goals? Are they aligned with what the Lord planned for your life when He wrote all your days in His book before you were born (see Day 1)?

Make today count, knowing this is the first day of the rest of your life. You can't change your destination overnight. Lay aside whatever distractions or weights are holding you back and pursue the Lord's will with all of your heart. You will find it if you seek with all your heart (Jer. 29:13).

Day 32

Hebrews 11:3

Through faith we understand that the worlds were framed by the word of God, so that things which are seen were not made of things which do appear.

Although people sometimes say poetically that God reached down with His hands and formed man of the dust of the ground, that's not what the Bible says. Genesis 1:3, 6, 9, 11, 14, 20, 24, and 26 all begin with "*And God said...*" Everything that exists was created when God spoke them into existence.

This is a very important truth.

Everything, physical or spiritual, was created by God's words. Therefore, God's words are the parent force. Everything created by His Word will respond to words. Speech is one of the things that sets man apart as being created in God's image (Gen. 1:26). We have power in our words (Prov. 18:21).

Modern man doesn't put much stock in words, as evidenced by all the litigation today. Even the words in contracts can be parsed and negated by charlatan lawyers. But God isn't like that. Psalm 89:34 says that every word that comes out of

God's mouth is a covenant or contract. It's impossible for God to lie (Heb. 6:18). He is bound by His Word.

Understanding the integrity of God's Word is necessary for faith because faith comes through hearing God's Word. If we don't know the power and integrity of God's Word, we can't take advantage of the tremendous power that is in it.

Today, look around you at this amazing world that God created and realize that everything you see was created by God's words. The same words that are written in your Bible created all things and revealed the promises that will create whatever you need if you mix them with faith (Heb. 4:2).

Hebrews 1:3

Who being the brightness of his *glory, and the express image of his person, and upholding all things by the word of his power, when he had by himself purged our sins, sat down on the right hand of the Majesty on high;*

Notice this is speaking of Jesus upholding all things by the word of his power. The Greek word that was translated "*upholding*" in this verse is *phero*, which means "to bear or carry." *The Message* Bible says, "*...He holds everything together by what he says—powerful words!*"

The nucleus of every atom is made up of all positively charged protons. Positively charged particles repel each other, just like how two positive ends or two negative ends of two magnets repel when they meet. This repulsion should make every atom fly apart, but some unseen force is holding them together.

Oral Roberts said that in a single slice of white bread, there is enough atomic energy to power an ocean liner across the Atlantic and back, but we don't know how to split those atoms. There are only a few unstable atoms, like uranium and plutonium that mankind has been able to split, releasing huge amounts of energy.

What is this unseen force that holds everything together? According to this verse, it's the power of God's spoken word. God spoke every atom in the universe into being, and they are held together by the power of His Word. If the Lord were to ever break His word, the universe would fly apart. That's the miraculous, unbreakable, miracle-working Word that we have been given in the Bible.

One word from Jesus, "*Come,*" was powerful enough to enable Peter to walk on the water (Matt. 14:29). "*Be thou clean*" was all it took to heal a leper (Matt. 8:3). "*Go*" is the only word Jesus spoke to cause thousands of demons to leave a man and enter into a whole herd of swine (Matt. 8:32). Jesus only spoke to a fig tree, and it died immediately (Mark 11:14).

Just imagine what God's Word can do for you today if you will mix faith with it (Heb. 4:2).

Day 34

Mark 4:14

The sower soweth the word.

Mark 4 records Jesus' parable about sowing seed on four different types of ground, only one of which produces fruit. Even then, there were varying amounts of fruit.

Notice, Jesus used a natural truth to teach a spiritual lesson about sowing God's Word in our hearts. If He had used a social system like school to illustrate sowing God's Word in your heart, it wouldn't have reflected this truth properly. You can cheat man-made systems, but you can't cheat on the law of sowing and reaping.

There is a God-created, natural law of seed, time, and then harvest. The time portion of this equation varies among seeds, but the formula is absolute. You can't have a harvest without sowing a seed and giving it time to germinate. Likewise, you can't reap a spiritual harvest without sowing the seed of God's Word in your heart and giving it time to mature.

A person would be crazy to just pray over the ground and expect it to produce food without sowing any seeds. But Christians do this all the time. They pray for healing, prosperity, or many other things without sowing the seeds from God's

Word in their hearts that would bring forth those results. You can fast and pray all you want, but you won't get fruit without planting the seed for the fruit that you want.

That's the way it is in the spiritual realm too. The laws that govern receiving from the Lord by sowing God's Word in your heart are absolutely essential to reaping the results you want. There are healing seeds, prosperity seeds, victory seeds, and seeds for whatever you need from the Lord. The problem isn't a lack of seeds in God's Word. The problem always lies with us not planting or protecting the seeds the Lord has given us.

Today, be as smart as a farmer: plant the seeds of God's Word in your heart and get ready for an abundant harvest. It's a law of God.

Mark 4:15

And these are they by the way side, where the word is sown; but when they have heard, Satan cometh immediately, and taketh away the word that was sown in their hearts.

In Jesus' parable, there were four types of ground that the seed fell upon, but only one type allowed the seed to produce a harvest. The first type of ground was a path where people had packed the ground down so hard that the seed couldn't penetrate below the surface. It just lay on top of the ground, and the birds came and ate it.

This compares spiritually to people whose hearts are hardened to God's Word, and the seed of God's Word never gets down inside them. That leaves it exposed to Satan, who has free access to steal God's Word from them. Sadly, many people today are in this category.

This same parable is recorded in Matthew 13:19, but Matthew says this first type of ground is symbolic of people who don't understand God's Word, and that's why the devil is able to steal it from them. So, understanding is the first step in getting God's Word down in your heart.

This is why we instruct children differently than adults. We don't change the truth. Truth is truth, and it works for all ages and cultures. But we must communicate truth in ways that people can relate to. That's why Jesus used a commonly understood truth about seeds to illustrate how God's Word works in our lives. Satan was only able to steal God's seed from those who didn't understand.

Jesus gave us the Holy Spirit to reveal truth to us (John 14:26 and 16:13). The Holy Spirit is the One who inspired men to write the Scriptures, so He will, therefore, reveal the truths contained in His Word. The Bible isn't written to your head. It's written to your heart, and you must read it with your heart, trusting the Holy Spirit to enlighten it to you (1 Cor. 2:14).

Ask the Lord to lead you into all truth and bring all the things He has said to you back to your remembrance (John 14:26). He wants to do that more than you want Him to do it. If you open your spiritual ears to hear, I believe the Lord will speak wonderful things out of His law to you (Ps. 119:18).

Mark 4:16–17

And these are they likewise which are sown on stony ground; who, when they have heard the word, immediately receive it with gladness; And have no root in themselves, and so endure but for a time: afterward, when affliction or persecution ariseth for the word's sake, immediately they are offended.

The second type of ground in Jesus' parable was descriptive of someone who got excited over God's Word, but they didn't give the Word of God time to get rooted in them. Therefore, they couldn't sustain the growth the seed produced. This is where I was when the Lord showed me this truth.

I got so excited over what I was hearing other ministers say that I couldn't contain it. I would bring back what I'd heard to my youth group to share with them, and it would produce fruit for a week or two. But this was in a Baptist church, and it wasn't received well by the leadership. They came against me, and I got offended just as this verse says, and the Word stopped having the same results.

I couldn't understand what was happening, but it happened so regularly that I came to expect it. I knew I would have to go back to get my spiritual batteries charged by listening to these other ministers, but it wouldn't last long. That's when the Lord revealed to me that I didn't have root in myself. I was trying to live off someone else's revelation.

In the same way that a seed must have enough depth of earth to put down roots, so we must have the Word of God rooted in our hearts in order to withstand the afflictions and persecutions the devil brings against us to steal away God's Word. I loved the truths I was learning, but I didn't have them rooted in my heart deep enough to withstand the onslaught that standing on the truth of God's Word brings. I was a shallow believer.

A typical tree has two to three times as much growth below ground as it does above ground. What takes place below ground in the invisible is what makes what we see in the visible possible. Likewise, the time we spend secretly with the Lord, getting His truths established in our hearts, isn't what people see, but we can't sustain growth without it.

Put a priority on letting God's Word take deep root in your heart.

Day 37

Mark 4:16–17

And these are they likewise which are sown on stony ground; who, when they have heard the word, immediately receive it with gladness; And have no root in themselves, and so endure but for a time: afterward, when affliction or persecution ariseth for the word's sake, immediately they are offended.

As I shared in yesterday's devotion, I had to make getting God's Word rooted in my heart the priority. I decided to make the truths I heard from others my very own. I determined I would never have to quote someone else, but I would let God's Word get so rooted in my life that it became my truth.

That was a major turning point in my life. I continued to listen to others, but it was different. I didn't just take what they said and run with it. I studied those things until the Lord confirmed them in my heart, and then I would meditate on those truths until they produced fruit in my own life.

Today, I don't minister things that aren't already bearing fruit in my life. I live what I teach before I teach it. If it's not working in me (bearing fruit), then I don't teach it to others. This is one reason why I haven't had to remove old teachings or go back and apologize for wrong teachings I've done. I don't just parrot what others say. I go to the source and get my revelations directly from the Lord.

Second Timothy 2:6 says, "*The husbandman that laboureth must be first partaker of the fruits.*" If what I'm laboring to share with others isn't working for me, then I don't need to be teaching it. This would stop a lot of wrong teaching if ministers would follow these guidelines.

This is not to say that everything in my life is working perfectly. If we wait until we arrive at perfection before we share God's Word, we'll never get there. I haven't arrived, but I've left. I'm still increasing in seeing the Lord supply my needs, but I've seen such supernatural results that I know the truths I'm sharing are correct. I'm not full grown, but I do have a good root system in God's Word.

Make the decision to take the truths you hear from others and go directly to the Lord and make them your own. Once those truths get rooted in your heart, no one will be able to take them from you.

Mark 4:16–17

And these are they likewise which are sown on stony ground; who, when they have heard the word, immediately receive it with gladness; And have no root in themselves, and so endure but for a time: afterward, when affliction or persecution ariseth for the word's sake, immediately they are offended.

Continuing from yesterday's devotional, you must have root in yourself to produce fruit. You can't depend on someone else to do this for you.

When I was in the sixth grade, my teacher illustrated how a seed must have roots by taking two identical terrariums and planting tomato seeds in them. Everything was identical, including the temperature and the way we cared for them, except for the amount of dirt. One terrarium had a couple of inches of dirt, while the other one had a foot of dirt. Can you guess which one sprouted first?

The one in shallow soil grew to nearly a foot tall before the other seed had even broken the ground. It had enough soil for the seed to sprout, but not enough for the seed to establish a good root system. It had to put its growth into the plant because there was no room to put down roots. The one in the shallow soil didn't have a root system that could sustain its growth. It turned white and withered just as the seed in the deep soil was beginning to sprout. The second seed grew tall and actually produced tomatoes while the other plant died. I learned a great lesson from that.

It takes time and a good root system to grow and sustain growth. We have been conditioned to want everything right now. We have microwaves, instant food, and fast food, and can buy nearly anything now and pay later. But it doesn't work that way in the kingdom of God. There is seed, t-i-m-e, and then harvest, which only a good root system can produce.

I encourage you to embrace the time it takes to get rooted in God's Word. Preparation time is never wasted time. The stronger your root system, the more fruit you will bear. You will pass up all the "flash in the pans" who took a truth and ran with it without being established enough to sustain their growth.

Good home cooking tastes better, but it takes longer to prepare. It's worth the wait.

Mark 4:16–17

And these are they likewise which are sown on stony ground; who, when they have heard the word, immediately receive it with gladness; And have no root in themselves, and so endure but for a time: afterward, when affliction or persecution ariseth for the word's sake, immediately they are offended.

Once again, I'm dealing with the second type of ground (heart) into which God's Word was sown. It started strong but was unable to produce any fruit. As Solomon said, "*Better* is *the end of a thing than the beginning thereof*" (Eccl. 7:8). Anyone can start, but it's how you finish that counts.

Notice that these verses reveal that afflictions and persecutions come "*for the word's sake.*" It's really not about us. The devil isn't afraid of us. It's God's Word that's a threat to his kingdom. He's coming against us to take our attention off God's Word.

It really bothered me that people in my church were criticizing me over what I was teaching. God made us for fellowship, and I think it's natural to want to get along with people. I was struggling with rejection from the people I loved and had been friends with for a long time.

During that time, I went to a meeting with about two hundred people in attendance. The speaker called me out of the crowd and prophesied that he saw me as a runner in a race. I was leading the race, but the people in the stands were telling me I was doing it all wrong. He saw me leave the track and go up into the grandstands to argue with the spectators. He said, "Even if you win the argument, you are going to lose the race." What a word picture!

That has become one of the most important things the Lord has ever spoken to me. Persecution isn't always bad. If you throw a rock into a pack of dogs, the one that yelps the loudest is the one that got hit. Those who persecute us the most are under conviction. But regardless of how loudly they yelp, we have to stay on track.

Make the determination that you aren't going to take your eyes off Jesus and His Word, regardless of what the people in the grandstands are yelling at you. You can't win the race if you are arguing with the spectators.

Day 40

Mark 4:18–19

And these are they which are sown among thorns; such as hear the word, And the cares of this world, and the deceitfulness of riches, and the lusts of other things entering in, choke the word, and it becometh unfruitful.

The third type of ground is something we have to contend with throughout our entire lifetime. This deals with other things occupying our attention so that we don't give the proper nourishment to God's Word.

We are not only spirit beings. We have a soul and live in a body. We have to give a certain amount of time and effort to physical, natural things to function in this world. However, God's Word must be the priority above everything else.

Like soil, we only have so much nourishment to give for things to grow in our lives. If weeds are allowed to grow unhindered, they will sap the moisture and minerals in our hearts that should go toward the plant we want.

We all want the biggest harvest possible in the spiritual realm, but are we pulling the weeds that would keep that from happening? This verse says the cares of this world, the deceitfulness of riches, and the lust of other things are like weeds that steal from the harvest we want. Not all of these things are sin, but they certainly don't help us grow the harvest we want. Hebrews 12:1 says to lay aside the weights and the sin which so easily besets us. Sins aren't the only thing that hinders us from winning the race. A runner with weights will not cross the finish line in first place.

I've even had the ministry act like a weed in my life. I'm called to this ministry. This is what the Lord wants for my life, but I can't let my ministry to others overshadow the Lord's ministry to me. I must put a priority on God's Word even above ministering to others. If that can happen to someone in the ministry, then it can certainly happen to anyone working a secular job or doing something that isn't sin, but it's choking the time God's Word needs in your life.

Take extra time today to meditate on God's Word and let something else, that may not be sin, go by the wayside so that the seed of God's Word will have your full attention. It will help you produce fruit one hundredfold.

Mark 4:20

And these are they which are sown on good ground; such as hear the word, and receive it, *and bring forth fruit, some thirtyfold, some sixty, and some an hundred.*

What made this fourth type of ground good? Did it have more than the other types of ground? No, it actually had less. It has less hard-packed ground, less rocks, and less weeds. If the key to bearing fruit is being less, then I can do that. I'm not sure I can be more, but I know I can be less.

God isn't looking for a silver vessel. He just wants a surrendered vessel. *The Lord is looking for someone who is committed to His Word above everything else!*

Did you notice that only one type of ground brought fruit to completion? That means, according to this parable, only one-fourth of people who encounter God's Word have it produce the fruit the Lord desires. That wasn't because of the seed. God's Word is an incorruptible seed (1 Pet. 1:23). The seed is never the problem. It's the ground that determines the return of the seed. You can have as much fruit as you are willing to commit to.

Jesus said in John 15:1–16 that He has ordained us to bring forth much fruit. It glorifies the Lord for us to be fruitful, but that doesn't happen automatically. We have to cultivate the soil of our hearts to remove everything hindering the seed of God's Word from producing.

Prayer without the faith and direction of God's Word can do more harm than good. Fasting is good, but if it is done to move God (which is contrary to what God's Word teaches), then all you are going to get is hungry. Nothing in this life compares with the power God's Word is meant to release in our lives.

As Romans 3:4 says, "*Let God be true, but every man a liar.*" I can expound on that to say, "Let God's Word be more important and dominate every other voice, including your own."

Today, the devil will try to keep you from understanding, getting rooted in, and putting God's Word first place in your life. Don't give in to any of those things. Exalt God's Word and it will exalt you.

Mark 4:31–33

> It is *like a grain of mustard seed, which, when it is sown in the earth, is less than all the seeds that be in the earth: But when it is sown, it groweth up, and becometh greater than all herbs, and shooteth out great branches; so that the fowls of the air may lodge under the shadow of it.*

I will never forget the first time the Lord spoke directly to me through these verses.

It was my first week in Vietnam in January of 1971. I was chosen to be the bunker guard while everyone else went through the gas chamber. I don't have the words to tell you how much I hated that part of our training. I begged the Lord to get me out of going through that again. Hallelujah! He did it. So, I was lying on my bunk, praising the Lord while all my peers were being gassed. What a deal!

I ran across this passage where the Lord compared the Word of God to a mustard seed, which grew into a huge tree that gave shelter to the fowls of the air from all over the earth. That's what I wanted. I was dreaming of having a ministry that touched people all over the world.

So, while I was imagining myself being this huge tree, the Lord spoke to me very clearly and said, "If I were to grant you the growth you are dreaming of right now, your root is only an inch deep. The first puff of wind or the first bird to land on one of your branches would topple the whole tree."

Wow! That wasn't what I wanted to hear. It really didn't bless me, but I knew it was the Lord, and it made an indelible impression on me. If I would just let God's Word take root in me, the growth above ground would come automatically.

Praise God! That became a directive from the Lord for the rest of my life. To this day, I'm still focused on the roots, and any good thing that has happened in or through me has come as a direct result of this.

The same will work for anyone who works it. God's Word is an incorruptible seed that will produce a huge tree if the roots are allowed to develop.

Day 43

Mark 4:26–27

And he said, So is the kingdom of God, as if a man should cast seed into the ground; And should sleep, and rise night and day, and the seed should spring and grow up, he knoweth not how.

This is yet another parable of Jesus from Mark 4 where He compares the Word of God to a seed. This must be important.

Verse 27 says the man who sowed the seed slept and rose night and day. This is describing time. It takes time for the seed of God's Word to produce fruit in our lives.

I knew a farmer who said he was the worst sinner in the whole county, but when he received salvation, he became a fanatical evangelist. He got so busy with sharing his testimony, that he missed the time to sow his seeds.

Since he was doing the Lord's work, he thought he would just sow his fields when he had a break in his schedule. So, he took out a half-million-dollar loan and sowed multiple sections of land with wheat seeds just a matter of weeks before harvest time. Of course, his seed didn't come up, and he just couldn't understand why he didn't get a harvest.

He knew he missed the proper time to plant his seed, but he thought the Lord would make his crop come up supernaturally since he was busy sharing his testimony. I'm sure you know it doesn't work that way. There is a time to sow and a time to reap (Eccl. 3:1-2). He missed the time to sow.

Many Christians do a similar thing without realizing it. They wait until they are in a crisis to turn to God's Word and start sowing seeds. They expect a harvest overnight and then get upset with the Lord when their answer doesn't come immediately. However, it takes time for God's Word to produce the fruit we want in our lives.

We need to faithfully sow the seed of God's Word in our hearts *before* we need to reap a harvest from it. I encourage you to put God's Word in your heart before you need it. Then, when you have a need, all you have to do is reap the harvest on the seeds you've already sown.

Day 44

Mark 4:28

For the earth bringeth forth fruit of herself; first the blade, then the ear, after that the full corn in the ear.

This continues the parable of the man casting seed into the ground and giving it time to grow before the harvest (Mark 4:26-30).

One of the most important things that the Lord ever showed me is that "*the earth* [brings] *forth fruit of herself.*" The Greek word *automatos,* which was translated "*of herself*" in this verse means "self-moved (automatic), i.e. spontaneous."[9] It is the root of our English words "automatic" and "automatically." The earth automatically releases the potential of whatever seed is planted in it.

Dirt doesn't discriminate. You can plant wheat seeds or tare seeds, and the ground will automatically start bringing the miracle potential out of that seed into the appropriate plant or tree. Likewise, our hearts just take whatever we put in it and make it come to pass.

This process works against us when we let the negative seeds of doubt and fear come into our hearts. That relates to the weeds in the Parable of the Sower that choked out the good plant in Mark 4:19. We can't let the ungodly seeds this world tries to sow in us every day take root. We must root them out like weeds.

But this same process will work for us if we let the incorruptible seed of God's Word abide in us. It's automatic or spontaneous. Given time, our hearts will release the supernatural power of God's Word if we keep the Word in the midst of our hearts (Prov. 4:20-22).

God made our hearts like dirt. The heart will produce whatever is sown in it. If we sow to the flesh, we will of the flesh reap corruption, but if we sow to the Spirit, we will of the Spirit reap life everlasting (Gal. 6:8).

We are programmed by the Lord to grow whatever is sown in our hearts. Therefore, we need to guard our hearts with all diligence and only put God's seeds in there. We will reap a harvest in time.

It's automatic.

Mark 4:28

For the earth bringeth forth fruit of herself; first the blade, then the ear, after that the full corn in the ear.

There is another very important lesson in this verse.

Notice that the earth brings forth fruit of herself. This is contrary to what most people think. Most people would say the seed is what brings forth the fruit, but this verse says it's the dirt that does that.

I've heard people say, "Anyone can count the number of seeds in an apple, but no one can count the number of apples in a seed." I understand the point they are making, but this verse says it's the earth that brings forth fruit, not the seed.

Seeds are a catalyst that activates the nutrients in the ground, and the ground is what produces the fruit. If the ground is barren, it won't produce fruit even though it has a perfect seed planted in it. God placed a miracle in seeds that causes the ground to produce fruit.

The benefit of this truth to us is that our born-again hearts are perfect and, like the good soil, have everything in them to bring forth fruit. It just needs a seed from God's Word to activate that process.

This fits perfectly with 1 Peter 1:23, where the Word of God is called an incorruptible seed. The Greek word translated "*seed*" in that verse is *spora*, which is a derivative of the Greek word *sperma*, where we get our English word "sperm" from.[10]

God's Word is a miraculous sperm that causes our hearts to bring forth fruit of herself. Notice this verse used the feminine gender to refer to the earth.

Just as the Lord created a woman with everything needed to produce a child except the sperm, so our born-again hearts have everything we need to produce fruit except the seed of God's Word.

Let the Lord's Word dwell in your heart, and it's just a matter of time until you give birth to your miracle.

Day 46

Mark 4:28

For the earth bringeth forth fruit of herself; first the blade, then the ear, after that the full corn in the ear.

Notice that there are stages of growth before the full harvest comes. This is very important.

Many people who are praying for the Lord's perfect will to come into their lives don't understand it is a process, just like the "*good, acceptable, and perfect will of God*" in Romans 12:2. If we don't understand the process, we will become frustrated or discouraged when we don't see our fruit produced instantly.

You can't survive going from zero to 100 mph instantly. That's not acceleration. That's a wreck, and it would kill you. But you can go 100 mph if you gradually accelerate up to that speed.

When the Lord shows me a long-term goal, I don't try to accomplish it all at once. I look for smaller, incremental steps toward that goal. "*But the path of the just* is *as the shining light, that shineth more and more unto the perfect day*" (Prov. 4:18).

You can't eat an elephant in one bite, but you could eat an elephant one bite at a time. Likewise, you can't accomplish God's perfect will, or get "*the full corn in the ear,*" as this parable calls it, all at once. There are always steps and stages in fulfilling God's will.

In 2000, after thirty-two years in ministry, the Lord told me I was just beginning my ministry as I started on television. That was discouraging and encouraging all at the same time. It meant that everything I had done up to that point was just preparation. I'd seen great times happen, so if I was just getting started, there were better things ahead. That has proven to be true in my life.

If you know where the Lord wants you to go, don't look so far ahead that you stumble over the steps the Lord has put in your path today. Ask the Lord to show you something you can do now that moves you in that direction. He wants you to go. Inch by inch, it's a cinch.

Day 47

Mark 4:29

But when the fruit is brought forth, immediately he putteth in the sickle, because the harvest is come.

Most of the teaching from these parables has been about the planting and the time it takes for the seed to germinate and bring forth fruit. As important as those truths are, the goal of all of this is the harvest. If a farmer did all the steps correctly but didn't harvest his crop at the right time, it would all be in vain.

I used to pastor a group of custom combiners. They would follow the wheat harvest from south Texas up into Wyoming. When the conditions were right for harvest, they would sometimes work twenty-four hours a day without a break to bring it in. You couldn't let the harvest just sit in the field. It had to be harvested at just the right time, or you would lose it.

Likewise, there is a time to sow and a time to reap in the spiritual realm too. We can't be so focused on the sowing and waiting time that we miss the right time to harvest. After all, that's the goal.

I've passed miles and miles of wheat fields in Kansas and Nebraska, and it's beautiful to see those stalks blowing in the breeze. I'm sure the farmers who planted those crops enjoy seeing that too. But just looking at the wheat is not why they went to all that effort. They want to harvest those crops and get them in the silos.

If they reap too soon, they don't get the full crop, and if they harvest too late, their crop may rot or be eaten by animals. They have to recognize the right time to harvest and make the most of it.

Likewise, there is an exact moment when the Word of God we've sown in our hearts comes to fruition, and we must recognize that moment and take advantage of it. It's possible to sow, fertilize, and weed our fields without reaping a harvest. The seed sown will germinate and grow to harvest automatically, but the harvest is dependent upon us recognizing it's harvest time and bringing it in.

Don't just sow God's Word in your heart. Expect it to bring forth fruit and recognize the harvest when it comes.

Psalm 138:2

I will worship toward thy holy temple, and praise thy name for thy lovingkindness and for thy truth: for thou hast magnified thy word above all thy name.

God's word is exalted even above His name! **What an amazing statement!**

At the name of Jesus every knee will bow, and every tongue confess that Jesus is Lord (Phil. 2:10–11). God's name is a strong tower of refuge (Prov. 18:10). Yet His word is even greater than His name.

A man's name is only as good as his word. Those who don't keep their word cannot be trusted. A godly person will keep their word even if it works to their detriment (Ps. 15:4).

The Lord cannot lie (Heb. 6:18). It's against His nature. If He ever broke His word, the universe would fly apart (Heb. 1:3). Therefore, we can take the Lord at His word and trust His promises completely.

The type of faith that made Jesus marvel was a faith in the power of His spoken word (Matt. 8:8–10). The centurion didn't have to have Jesus physically come to his house. If He would just speak the word, he believed his servant would be healed.

One word from Jesus, "*Come,*" was enough to allow Peter to walk on the water (Matt. 14:29). Jesus cast out demons and healed the sick with only His word (Matt. 8:16). Jesus spoke everything that exists into existence by His words (Gen. 1). He framed the worlds by His words (Heb. 11:3).

The Bible is a compilation of millions of words from God that provide us with knowledge that allows us to partake of His divine nature (2 Pet. 1:4). We must understand that God is not a man who can lie (Num. 23:19). All lies originate from the devil (John 8:44). God's Word can be trusted.

What a blessing to have God's Word available to us today. Many people have sacrificed their lives to make this possible because they understood that faith comes by hearing God's Word (Rom. 10:17).

I encourage you to put God's Word first place in your life today. If we exalt the truths of God's Word, they will exalt us and open up the miraculous power of God to flow through us.

Day 49

Hosea 4:6

My people are destroyed for lack of knowledge....

There are only three things that can keep the power of God's Word from working in our lives: a lack of knowing what God's Word says (Hos. 4:6), traditions and doctrines of men (Mark 7:13), and not mixing faith with God's Word (Heb. 4:2). These are things that are totally within our control.

First, ignorance of God's Word is devastating. People often say, "Ignorance is bliss," but that's not true. What we don't know is killing us.

Look at the laws of nature. Electricity has been here since the first day of creation. People could have been using electricity since day one if they had known the laws that govern it, but it has only been relatively recently that we've learned how to harness that power. How our lives would be different without it.

Or look at the laws that govern flight. Men could have been flying airplanes thousands of years ago if they had known the laws of aerodynamics. Think of how that could have changed history. Mankind might have already been traveling to other planets and solar systems by now.

Think of the millions of lives that could have been saved from premature death if they had known just the basic laws of hygiene that are commonly practiced today. Who knows what inventions would have been discovered if men had lived long enough to follow through on their ideas?

Likewise, God's people are perishing today from the ignorance that comes from not having a revelation of God's Word. God's Word is the key to health, happiness, prosperity, success, and everything that pertains to life and godliness (2 Pet. 1:3).

Make the commitment today to not be ignorant any longer. All of God's treasures are hidden for us in His Word. Seek for them like you would seek for gold. You won't be disappointed.

Mark 7:13

Making the word of God of none effect through your tradition, which ye have delivered: and many such like things do ye.

Not knowing what God's Word says will keep us from receiving its benefit, but so will wrong knowledge or religious traditions.

Ignorance of God's Word is like a blank whiteboard. The remedy for that is to write the truths of God's Word on it. But wrong doctrine is like having a whiteboard that is full of junk. You have to erase all the lies before you can write the truth on there.

All of us have had our whiteboards (minds) filled with junk. We've been raised in a fallen world that teaches values completely contrary to God's Word. Even those raised in church have lots of beliefs that don't square with God's Word. I certainly did.

I was told that God is the one who killed my dad when I was just twelve years old. The pastor said the Lord needed my dad in heaven more than I did. I was told that the Lord sovereignly controlled everything, and I had to just roll with the punches. Prosperity, healing, miracles, and all the power that the first century church walked in had passed away and wasn't for us anymore.

All those things are doctrines of men that make the Word of God of no effect. The Bible is the antidote for all these lies that have negated the power of God in so many people's lives.

It's easier to take a person who knows nothing and educate them in the truth of God's Word than it is to take a person who has been taught wrong and reprogram their thinking. But regardless of which situation you may find yourself in, the answer is the same. God's Word is truth (John 17:17), and knowing the truth will set you free (John 8:32).

A true revelation of truth that comes only from God's Word is the single most important thing you can do to experience God and the good things He has planned for your life.

Don't delay. Make knowing the Lord through His Word your priority today.

Hebrews 4:2

> *For unto us was the gospel preached, as well as unto them: but the word preached did not profit them, not being mixed with faith in them that heard* it.

The third thing that will stop the power of God's Word from working in your life is not mixing God's Word with faith. We can see that with the Israelites who came out of Egypt. He had great plans to bring them into the Promised Land that flowed with milk and honey, but they died in the wilderness.

Why? It was because they didn't mix faith with the words that the Lord gave them. They chose to believe the "Ten Spies Network," which focused on the giants and walled cities instead of the "Two Spies Report," which said they were well able to take these cities (Num. 13).

The unbelieving ten spies told the people there were giants. That was a fact—there *were* giants—but the truth of God's Word trumps facts. God promised them that no man would be able to stand before them (Deut. 7:24 and 11:25). They would have easily conquered the land if they had just believed what the Lord told them.

Forty years later, Rahab told the two spies whom Joshua sent into Jericho that the day they heard about the Lord drying up the Red Sea and slaying all the Egyptians (Ex. 14:29–30), all the men's hearts fainted, and their strength left them (Josh. 2:9–11). If the people had received the report of the two faithful spies instead of the ten negative spies, taking the Promised Land would have been a "cakewalk."

Sure, there will always be giants between us and victory, but the bigger the giant, the greater the victory. Nobody would have praised David if he had killed a dwarf. They would have arrested him.

What promises has the Lord given you? Are you listening to the "Ten Spies Network" tell you about all the giants or are you looking at God's promises of victory?

Faith only comes through hearing God's Word (Rom. 10:17). Take a promise of God, let it give you faith, and your miracle is on the way.

Matthew 11:4–6

Jesus answered and said unto them, Go and shew John again those things which ye do hear and see: The blind receive their sight, and the lame walk, the lepers are cleansed, and the deaf hear, the dead are raised up, and the poor have the gospel preached to them. And blessed is he, *whosoever shall not be offended in me.*

This records John sending two of his disciples to Jesus to ask if He was the Christ. This is a big deal!

John had boldly proclaimed that Jesus was the Lamb of God who takes away the sins of the world (John 1:29 and 36). God told John that when he saw the Holy Spirit visibly descend on someone, it was a sign that the person was the Christ (John 1:33). John also heard the audible voice of God say that Jesus was His beloved Son, in whom He was well pleased (Matt. 3:17). John at one time *knew* Jesus was the Messiah. Thus, John said Jesus must increase, but he must decrease (John 3:30).

But after being locked up in prison, John doubted that he had anointed the right one to be the Messiah. John had no life outside of God's calling. John was filled with the Holy

Spirit while still in his mother's womb (Luke 1:41). He never married, had kids, or had any purpose outside of announcing the Messiah to the nation. If he pointed everyone to the wrong man, his life would have been wasted. This was a big deal to John.

How did Jesus respond when John sent his disciples to ask for help? For starters, He didn't respond for about an hour (Luke 7:21–23). He just went about healing people and then told John's disciples to go tell John what they had seen and heard, and that he would be blessed if he wasn't offended.

Jesus' response bothered me for many years. John was in a crisis, and it didn't seem like Jesus responded in kind. I thought John would have been blessed much more by what Jesus said about him after his disciples left than by just telling him what they saw and heard.

I'll deal with what Jesus was really doing more in tomorrow's devotion, but today, realize that even John doubted. He had audible and visible manifestations that should have taken away his doubts, but they didn't. If John could doubt, so can you. God's Word is the only true antidote to unbelief.

Day 53

Isaiah 35:5–6

Then the eyes of the blind shall be opened, and the ears of the deaf shall be unstopped. Then shall the lame man *leap as an hart, and the tongue of the dumb sing:*

Yesterday, I showed even John the Baptist struggled with doubt. Negative circumstances have a way of shaking our faith. John was in a crisis, asking Jesus for help.

Jesus ignored John's messengers for an hour and then told them to tell John what they had seen and heard and not to be offended. After John's disciples left, Jesus said John was the greatest man who had ever lived (Matt. 11:11). That put him above Moses, David, Elijah, Isaiah, Daniel, and all the other Old Testament greats.

Why would Jesus say all those wonderful things after John's disciples left (Luke 7:24)? Wouldn't John have been encouraged to hear all these wonderful things Jesus said about him?

Isaiah 35 prophesied that the Messiah would open the eyes of the blind and unstop deaf ears. The lame man would leap like a deer, and He would cause the mute to speak. That's exactly what Jesus did and told John's messengers to report that to him. Jesus fulfilled exactly what Isaiah said He would do and even added raising someone from the dead, just so there would be no mistake that He was the Christ. Wow!

Jesus responded to John, but not in the way most of us would want. When we struggle with unbelief, most of us want a hug. We want something emotional that would help us with our feelings. But feelings aren't faith.

Faith only comes by hearing God's Word (Rom. 10:17). Jesus pointed John back to the very scriptures the Lord had used to instruct him about what the Messiah would do. He sent him back to the Word. That's where our faith comes from.

It's because Jesus loved and esteemed John so much that He didn't just give him an emotional fix. He gave John His Word, which I'm sure brought him back into faith and allowed him to go out with a shout.

What are you looking for? Are you wanting an emotional fix or world-overcoming faith? The choice is yours (Deut. 30:19).

Hebrews 4:12

For the word of God is *quick, and powerful, and sharper than any twoedged sword, piercing even to the dividing asunder of soul and spirit, and of the joints and marrow, and* is *a discerner of the thoughts and intents of the heart.*

The Bible is not like any other book. It's alive and life-giving!

However, I read the Bible daily for years before it came alive to me. I could even quote many verses from the Bible, but they didn't change my life.

Then I had an encounter with the Lord in 1968, where I was filled with the Holy Spirit, and all that changed. It felt like I couldn't open the Bible without the Lord yelling at me. God's Word became like fire in my bones, and I couldn't help but tell everyone what He was saying to me (Jer. 20:9).

The Bible is a supernaturally inspired book (2 Pet. 1:21), and without the Holy Spirit's help, it's a closed book. The Lord hasn't hidden these truths from us but for us. The key to unlocking the Bible's power is having the One who wrote it (the Holy Spirit) quicken it to our hearts. It wasn't written to our heads but to our hearts.

First Corinthians 2:14 says that our natural minds can't receive the things of the Spirit of God. We can only understand and release this power when we open our hearts and let the Holy Spirit reveal the true meaning of what He inspired.

After Jesus rose from the dead, He expounded to two of His disciples on the road to Emmaus all the prophecies in the Old Testament about Him and what He came to accomplish (Luke 24:13-31). They said, "*Did not our heart burn within us, while he talked with us by the way, and while he opened to us the scriptures?*" (Luke 24:32).

Later that same day, Jesus opened their understanding so that they might understand the scriptures (Luke 24:45). That's what each of us needs to have happen in our lives, and the good news is that Jesus wants to do this more than we want it.

Today, open your heart. Ask the Holy Spirit to speak to your heart by revelation, and I believe God's Word will start a fire in your heart.

2 Peter 1:3

According as his divine power hath given unto us all things that pertain *unto life and godliness, through the knowledge of him that hath called us to glory and virtue:*

What a powerful statement! Everything that pertains to life and godliness comes through the knowledge of God. Any lack in any area of our lives reveals a lack of the true knowledge of God.

I can just hear people saying, "No, I don't have a lack of knowledge. I've got a lack of money or healing." But there are scriptures that promise us financial prosperity, and healing, and everything else we need. Just as Peter said, everything we need comes through the knowledge of God.

In the late 1990s, I knew the Lord wanted me to go on TV, but I was afraid that I couldn't afford it. I had been on radio for twenty-five years and struggled to pay my bills. How could I ever afford TV, which was a hundred times more expensive? I knew I had to have a breakthrough.

I took about a hundred scriptures on financial prosperity and began to meditate on them. I didn't go to someone else's book and copy scriptures they had on prosperity. I already knew these verses, but my lack of prosperity showed me that I didn't have a true revelation of what the Lord was saying.

So, after two years of doing that, it's like a bomb went off on the inside of me. Suddenly, a supernatural faith rose up in my heart (Rom. 10:17), and I had a breakthrough.

Prior to that time, I would hold three-day meetings, and my offerings would be within five or ten dollars of breaking even with the expenses. After that revelation, I started receiving two or three times as much money in the offerings as my expenses.

The only thing that changed was my heart. Everything else about these meetings was the same. It was my heart that changed because of the knowledge of God that came through meditating on His Word day and night.

It's the same for you. God's Word contains His knowledge. It's the key to receiving whatever you need. Devour God's Word today.

2 Peter 1:4

Whereby are given unto us exceeding great and precious promises: that by these ye might be partakers of the divine nature, having escaped the corruption that is in the world through lust.

Yesterday's devotion focused on the fact that everything that pertains to life and godliness comes through the knowledge of God. This verse shows us how to acquire this knowledge. It's found in God's Word.

The "*whereby*" in this verse is speaking about God's knowledge. That's what gave us all these exceeding great and precious promises. The Bible reveals God's thoughts, standards, and ways to us. We wouldn't know how to spell Jesus if it weren't for the Bible.

Outside of Jesus coming and redeeming us, then leaving the Holy Spirit here to indwell us, the greatest gift God ever gave mankind is the Bible. It reveals who He is, what He has done, and what He wants to do in our lives. The Bible reveals that God is love (1 John 4:8 and 16). The Bible is God's love letter to us.

This verse goes on to say that a true revelation of God's Word is how we partake of His divine nature and escape the corruption that is in the world through lust. That's awesome!

Do you need to escape from something the world has thrown at you or overcome its lusts? Of course, we all do. And the way to accomplish this is through the exceedingly great and precious promises of God's Word.

It's like the Lord has thrown us a lifesaver. If we would just grab hold of His Word and meditate in it day and night, it will change us effortlessly. It will cleanse us and keep us from sin (Ps. 119:9 and 11). It will be a lamp unto our feet and a light to our path (Ps. 119:105).

The provision has been made. The Lord hasn't left us on our own. We have His Word, but it's our responsibility to put it in our hearts. The seed of God's Word won't jump off the page without us putting it before our eyes.

Lord, open my eyes to behold wondrous things out of Your law (Ps. 119:18).

Joshua 1:8

This book of the law shall not depart out of thy mouth; but thou shalt meditate therein day and night, that thou mayest observe to do according to all that is written therein: for then thou shalt make thy way prosperous, and then thou shalt have good success.

Everyone wants prosperity and good success, but few are willing to do what this verse says we have to do. We must meditate in God's Word, day and night, to observe and do all that is written therein. Then, and only then, will we experience the prosperity and success this verse promises.

This verse needs to be interpreted in light of our new and better covenant (Heb. 8:6). We now have the whole of Scripture to meditate on, not just the first five books of the Bible as Joshua did. We also don't get what we deserve, like those under the Old Testament Law, but we get what Jesus purchased for us through faith in what He did and not what we do.

However, since faith comes by hearing God's Word (Rom. 10:17), we still need to be meditating in God's Word day and night to activate the faith necessary to appropriate what Jesus provided through His death and resurrection.

Although God isn't responding to our meditation, our meditation is essential to renewing our minds and activating the faith God gave us so we can respond to Him properly.

Prosperity and good success really are as simple as just meditating in God's Word day and night, but it isn't that easy. One of the hardest things you will ever do is refuse the knowledge of good and evil this world tempts us with every day and just commit to the truth of God's Word.

Second Corinthians 10:4–5 reveals the battle is in our minds, but the spiritual weapons the Lord has given us are mighty through God and will bring every thought into captivity and under obedience to Christ. You can live with your mind stayed on the Lord the whole time you are going about your daily tasks. It can be done, or the Lord wouldn't have told us to do it.

The Lord will keep you in perfect peace today as you keep your mind stayed upon Him (Isa. 26:3).

Psalm 1:2

...in his law doth he meditate day and night.

Psalm 2:1

Why do the heathen rage, and the people imagine a vain thing?

As we discussed in yesterday's devotion, meditating in God's Word is the key to prosperity and good success, but how do we do that? You can't just read the Bible all day, every day. Somebody has to work.

It's true, we can't read God's Word all day, every day. We all have responsibilities, but meditation is just going over and over what we have read in God's Word until it becomes visible in our heart's eye. We can do that while we are working, or driving, or whatever we need to do.

I'm sure you've worried all day over something, while you still went to work and got your job done. The part of you that worries is the same part that meditates. Worry is just meditating on what might or has already gone wrong.

The same Hebrew word that was translated "*meditate*" in Psalm 1:2 was translated "*imagine*" in Psalm 2:1. That's because the way you meditate is to imagine.

Instead of imagining negative things, you can imagine God's promises coming true in your life. You can't do that if you don't know what God has promised you or if you don't understand how the kingdom of God operates. That's why it is imperative that we know God's Word, front to back. It's our covenant or contract with Him. It's how He reveals Himself to us and how we learn what is ours in Christ.

But once we've put the information in us, the real power of God's Word is released when we see it in our hearts, which is what meditation accomplishes. We can see with our hearts what can't be seen with our physical eyes (2 Cor. 4:18). That's our imagination, and it involves meditating. No one is as blind as those who only see with their physical eyes

Meditate on this truth all day long as you go about your daily tasks. I believe you will experience a new level of understanding in God's Word as you set your mind on the things above.

Romans 8:6

"For to be carnally minded is *death; but to be spiritually minded* is *life and peace."*

If we are experiencing anything other than life and peace, it's because we aren't spiritually minded. That's tight, but it's right!

And what is being "*spiritually minded*"?

Jesus said His words are spirit, and they are life (John 6:63). Therefore, being spiritually minded is being Word-of-God-minded. If we focus on God's Word exclusively, all we will get is life and peace. Or as Isaiah said, "*Thou wilt keep* him *in perfect peace, whose mind is stayed on* thee: *because he trusteth in thee*" (Is. 26:3).

The word "*mind*" in Isaiah 26:3 was translated from the Hebrew word *yetser*, which means "a form, figuratively, conception (i.e. purpose)."[11] This same Hebrew word was translated "imagination" elsewhere in the Old Testament. Our minds, or more specifically, our imaginations, are where we conceive our miracles.

Are you praying for healing but thinking sick? Are you praying for prosperity but thinking poor? If so, you must change the image on the inside before you see it on the outside. You do that by meditating in God's Word until you can see yourself in victory.

If you can't see victory on the inside, you won't see it on the outside.

You can change that inner image by taking the promise of God's Word concerning your situation and meditating on it until you see yourself the way the Lord has promised in His Word. As you think in your heart, that's the way it will be (Prov. 23:7).

Today, take a promise from God's Word that addresses your situation and meditate on it all day long. Your mind may wander, but just bring it back to focus on that promise until you see yourself walking in the victory that promise provides. You may not accomplish this in one day, but you can't get to that place any quicker than to start right now. As long as it takes, continue to keep that promise in your imagination until you see it with your physical eyes. It will come.

Jeremiah 29:11

For I know the thoughts that I think toward you, saith the Lord, thoughts of peace, and not of evil, to give you an expected end.

A prominent minister once said that the place with the most potential in every community is the local graveyard. That's because many people die without having realized everything God had for them.

God is no respecter of persons (Acts 10:34). He wants to do absolutely miraculous things in everyone's life. We all have something that God wants to accomplish through us, but many people are ignorant of these things. People have just bought into the lie that there's nothing special about them. But the truth is that each of us is unique and can do something that nobody else can.

You may not feel like there's anything special about you, but God created you for something big. He has awesome plans toward you. The Bible says that God has "*an expected end*" for every person. Other translations say that He has a hope and a future for us.

God has good thoughts toward each of us. He has a perfect plan for our lives. We are fearfully and wonderfully made (Ps. 139:14–16). Whether our parents saw us coming or not, God knew us from the foundation of the world and has a purpose for us. Yet, most of us are living way below God's standard and limiting what He wants to do in our lives.

Life is not a dress rehearsal—this is the real thing. If you aren't doing something with your life that fulfills you, then you are not making the most out of your life. You are limiting God in that way. God has a purpose for you, and when you find it, you will be fulfilled.

We all have a sphere of influence, or people we can reach. These are people who know us and are watching us—family members, neighbors, friends, and coworkers—who will miss God's best for their lives if we just sit around and wait for our pastor or another minister to talk to them. We need to rise up and let God use us to touch these people and help us reach our full potential.

End Notes

1. *Strong's Definitions*, s.v. "םַקָר" ("*rāqam*"), accessed December 2, 2024, https://www.blueletterbible.org/lexicon/h7551/kjv/wlc/0-1/

2. *Strong's Definitions*, s.v. "םֶלֹ·ג" ("*gōlem*"), accessed December 2, 2024, https://www.blueletterbible.org/lexicon/h1564/kjv/wlc/0-1/

3. *Strong's Definitions*, s.v. "συσχηματίζω" ("*syschēmatizō*"), accessed December 3, 2024, https://www.blueletterbible.org/lexicon/g4964/kjv/tr/0-1/

4. *Vine's Expository Dictionary of New Testament Words*, s.v., "θεόπνευστος" ("*theopneustos*"), accessed January 28, 2025, https://www.blueletterbible.org/search/Dictionary/viewTopic.cfm?topic=VT0001509

5. *Strong's Definitions*, s.v. "μεταμορφόω" ("*metamorphoō*"), accessed December 3, 2024, https://www.blueletterbible.org/lexicon/g3339/kjv/tr/0-1/

6. *Strong's Definitions*, s.v. "ףַרָצ" ("*ṣārap̄*"), accessed December 3, 2024, https://www.blueletterbible.org/lexicon/h6884/kjv/wlc/0-1/

7. *Strong's Definitions*, s.v. "ὑπομονή" ("*hypomonē*"), accessed December 3, 2024, https://www.blueletterbible.org/lexicon/g5281/kjv/tr/0-1/

8. *Strong's Definitions*, s.v. "קָשַׁב" ("*qāšaḇ*"), accessed December 3, 2024, https://www.blueletterbible.org/lexicon/h7181/kjv/wlc/0-1/

9. *Strong's Definitions*, s.v. "α□τ□ματος" ("*automatos*"), accessed January 9, 2026, https://www.blueletterbible.org/lexicon/g844/kjv/tr/0-1/

10. *Blue Letter Bible*, s.v. "σπορ□" ("*spora*"), accessed January 9, 2026, https://www.blueletterbible.org/lexicon/g4701/kjv/tr/0-1/ and Blue Letter Bible, s.v. "σπ□ρμα" ("*sperma*"), accessed January 9, 2026, https://www.blueletterbible.org/lexicon/g4690/kjv/tr/0-1/

11. *Blue Letter Bible*, s.v. "יֵצֶר" ("*yetser*"), accessed January 9, 2026, https://www.blueletterbible.org/lexicon/h3336/kjv/wlc/0-1/

FURTHER STUDY

If you enjoyed this booklet and would like to learn more about some of the things I've shared, I suggest my teachings:

1. *How to Find, Follow, and Fulfill God's Will*
2. *Spirit, Soul & Body*
3. *You've Already Got It*
4. *Effortless Change*
5. *The Power of Imagination*

Plus 200,000 hours of free teaching on our website.

These teachings are available for free at **awmi.net**, or they can be purchased at **awmi.net/store**.

Go deeper in your relationship with God by browsing all of Andrew's free teachings.

Receive Jesus as Your Savior

Choosing to receive Jesus Christ as your Lord and Savior is the most important decision you'll ever make!

God's Word promises, "*That if thou shalt confess with thy mouth the Lord Jesus, and shalt believe in thine heart that God hath raised him from the dead, thou shalt be saved. For with the heart man believeth unto righteousness; and with the mouth confession is made unto salvation*" (Rom. 10:9–10). "*For whosoever shall call upon the name of the Lord shall be saved*" (Rom. 10:13). By His grace, God has already done everything to provide salvation. Your part is simply to believe and receive.

Pray out loud: "Jesus, I acknowledge that I've sinned and need to receive what you did for the forgiveness of my sins. I confess that You are my Lord and Savior. I believe in my heart that God raised You from the dead. By faith in Your Word, I receive salvation now. Thank You for saving me."

The very moment you commit your life to Jesus Christ, the truth of His Word instantly comes to pass in your spirit. Now that you're born again, there's a brand-new you!

Please contact us and let us know that you've prayed to receive Jesus as your Savior. We'd like to send you some free materials to help you on your new journey. Call our Helpline: **719-635-1111** (available 24 hours a day, seven days a week) to speak to a staff member who is here to help you understand and grow in your new relationship with the Lord.

Welcome to your new life!

Receive the Holy Spirit

As His child, your loving heavenly Father wants to give you the supernatural power you need to live a new life. *"For every one that asketh receiveth; and he that seeketh findeth; and to him that knocketh it shall be opened...how much more shall* your *heavenly Father give the Holy Spirit to them that ask him?"* (Luke 11:10–13).

All you have to do is ask, believe, and receive! Pray this: "Father, I recognize my need for Your power to live a new life. Please fill me with Your Holy Spirit. By faith, I receive it right now. Thank You for baptizing me. Holy Spirit, You are welcome in my life."

Some syllables from a language you don't recognize will rise up from your heart to your mouth (1 Cor. 14:14). As you speak them out loud by faith, you're releasing God's power from within and building yourself up in the spirit (1 Cor. 14:4). You can do this whenever and wherever you like.

It doesn't really matter whether you felt anything or not when you prayed to receive the Lord and His Spirit. If you believed in your heart that you received, then God's Word promises you did. *"Therefore I say unto you, What things soever ye desire, when ye pray, believe that ye receive* them, *and ye shall have* them" (Mark 11:24). God always honors His Word—believe it!

We would like to rejoice with you, pray with you, and answer any questions to help you understand more fully what has taken place in your life!

Please contact us to let us know that you've prayed to be filled with the Holy Spirit and to request the book *The New You & the Holy Spirit*. This book will explain in more detail about the benefits of being filled with the Holy Spirit and speaking in tongues. Call our Helpline: **719-635-1111** (available 24 hours a day, seven days a week).

Call for Prayer

If you need prayer for any reason, you can call our Helpline, 24 hours a day, seven days a week, at **719-635-1111**. A trained prayer minister will answer your call and pray with you.

Every day, we receive testimonies of healings and other miracles from our Helpline, and we are ministering God's nearly-too-good-to-be-true message of the Gospel to more people than ever. So, I encourage you to call today!

About the Author

Andrew Wommack's life was forever changed the moment he encountered the supernatural love of God on March 23, 1968. As a renowned Bible teacher and author, Andrew has made it his mission to change the way the world sees God.

Andrew's vision is to go as far and deep with the Gospel as possible. His message goes far through the *Gospel Truth* television program, which is available to over half the world's population. The message goes deep through discipleship at Charis Bible College, headquartered in Woodland Park, Colorado. Founded in 1994, Charis has campuses across the United States and around the globe.

Andrew also has an extensive library of teaching materials in print, audio, and video. More than 200,000 hours of free teachings can be accessed at **awmi.net**.

Contact Information

Andrew Wommack Ministries, Inc.

PO Box 3333
Colorado Springs, CO 80934-3333
info@awmi.net
awmi.net

Helpline: 719-635-1111 (available 24/7)

Charis Bible College

info@charisbiblecollege.org
844-360-9577
CharisBibleCollege.org

For international offices,
visit **awmi.net/contact-us**.

Connect with us on social media.

Andrew Wommack's *Living Commentary* digital study Bible is a user-friendly, downloadable program. It's like reading the Bible with Andrew at your side, sharing his revelation with you verse by verse.

Main features:

- Bible study software with a grace-and-faith perspective
- Over 27,000 notes by Andrew on verses from Genesis through Revelation
- *Adam Clarke's Commentary on the Bible*
- *Albert Barnes' Notes on the Whole Bible*
- *Matthew Henry's Concise Commentary*
- 12 Bible versions
- 3 optional premium translation add-ons: *New Living Translation*, *New International Version*, and *The Message* (additional purchase of $9.99 each)
- 2 concordances: *Englishman's Concordance* and *Strong's Concordance*
- 2 dictionaries: *Collaborative International Dictionary* and *Holman's Dictionary*
- Atlas with biblical maps
- Bible and *Living Commentary* statistics
- Quick navigation, including history of verses
- Robust search capabilities (for the Bible and Andrew's notes)
- "Living" (i.e., constantly updated and expanding)
- Ability to create personal notes
- Accessible online and offline

Whether you're new to studying the Bible or a seasoned Bible scholar, you'll gain a deeper revelation of the Word from a grace-and-faith perspective.

Purchase Andrew's *Living Commentary* today at **awmi.net/living** and grow in the Word with Andrew.

Item code: 8350

ANDREW WOMMACK MINISTRIES

***God Wants You Well* book**

In this book, Andrew reveals the truth of what God's unconditional love and grace has already provided. Healing is a big part of that provision. So why does religion tell you that God uses sickness to teach you something? It even tries to make you believe that sickness is a blessing. That's just not true! God wants you well! If you or someone you know needs healing, this book is for you.

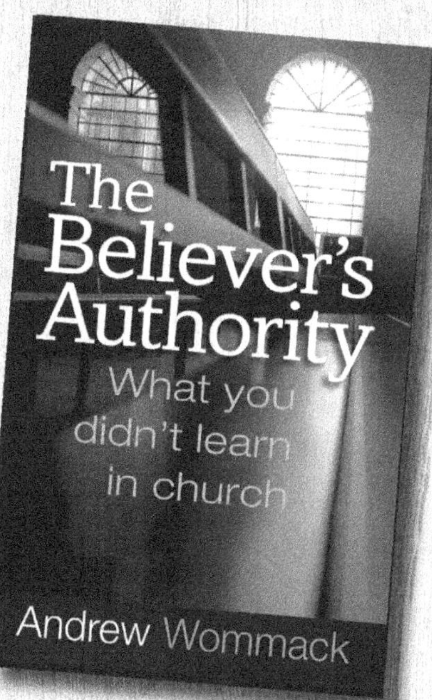

***The Believer's Authority* book**

Dig into the scriptures with Andrew as he uncovers the spiritual significance of your choices, words, and actions. He explores how they affect your ability to stand against the attacks of Satan and to receive God's best. Discover the powerful truths behind true spiritual authority and begin seeing real results.

www.ingramcontent.com/pod-product-compliance
Lightning Source LLC
LaVergne TN
LVHW020633100826
845148LV00012B/2169